THE 1 _,\I°

Teachers are the most important determinant of the quality of schools. We should be doing everything we can to help them get better.

In recent years, however, a cocktail of box-ticking demands, ceaseless curriculum reform, disruptive reorganisations and an audit culture that requires teachers to document their every move, have left the profession deskilled and demoralised. Instead of rolling out the red carpet for teachers, we have been pulling it from under their feet.

The result is predictable: there is now a cavernous gap between the quantity and quality of teachers we need, and the reality in our schools.

In this book, Rebecca Allen and Sam Sims draw on the latest research from economics, psychology and education to explain where the gap came from and how we can close it again. Including interviews with current and former teachers, as well as end-of-chapter practical guidance for schools, The Teacher Gap sets out how we can better recruit, train and retain the next generation of teachers.

At the heart of the book is a simple message: we need to give teachers a career worth having.

Rebecca Allen is Professor of Education and Director of the Centre for Education Improvement Science (CEIS) at the UCL Institute of Education, UK. She was previously the Founding Director of Education Datalab, and is an expert in the analysis of large scale administrative and survey datasets. You can find Becky on Twitter @profbeckyallen

Sam Sims is a Research Fellow at Education Datalab and a PhD researcher at UCL Institute of Education, UK. He researches teachers and education policy and has a particular interest in how teachers' working environments affect their professional development. You can find him on Twitter @Sam_Sims_

THE TEACHER GAP

Rebecca Allen and Sam Sims

LONDON AND NEW YORK

First published 2018
by Routledge
2 Park Square, Milton Park, Abingdon, Oxon OX14 4RN

and by Routledge
711 Third Avenue, New York, NY 10017

Routledge is an imprint of the Taylor & Francis Group, an informa business

British Library Cataloguing in Publication Data
A catalogue record for this book is available from the British Library

Library of Congress Cataloging in Publication Data
A catalog record for this book has been requested

ISBN: 978-1-138-73088-5 (hbk)
ISBN: 978-1-138-73089-2 (pbk)
ISBN: 978-1-315-18922-2 (ebk)

Typeset in Aldus Roman and Scala Sans
by Florence Production Ltd, Stoodleigh, Devon, UK

MIX
Paper from
responsible sources
FSC   FSC® C013056
www.fsc.org

Printed and bound in Great Britain by
TJ International Ltd, Padstow, Cornwall

Sam: To my wife, parents and teachers, without whom I could never have written this book.

Becky: To my mother Jill, who has taught me more about what it means to be a teacher than anyone else; and to my husband Ian, for looking after Juliet and Eddie while I wrote this book.

CONTENTS

CONTENTS

ACKNOWLEDGEMENTS

Thank you to all the teachers we interviewed for this book. Although most of you appear as pseudonyms in the text, we are personally very grateful to each of you for sharing your experiences with us. Your honesty and frankness has added insight and helped humanise the cold, hard research.

Thanks to reviewers of earlier book drafts, whose comments have improved the final version: Caroline Barlow, Keven Bartle, Ian Bauckham, Simon Burgess, Cat Carter, Leora Cruddas, Harry Fletcher-Wood, Matthew Hood, Rebecca Lynch, Peps McCrea, Laura McInerney, Alison Peacock and Stephen Tierney. Particular thanks go to the three anonymous reviewers for your detailed and helpful feedback. Any errors remain those of the authors.

CHAPTER ONE

The teacher gap

Education is unique among the public services in its ability to propel people forward. Health care, social care and policing are, of course, vital. But they focus on protecting people from risk or putting them back on their feet after misfortune. Only education gives us the power to go further. Learning is a source of dignity and an important element of human flourishing. Hard data now shows that it also makes us richer, healthier and happier.[1] Improving education is therefore the holy grail of public policy.

But almost one hundred years since secondary education became a right for every child in England, a good education is still not a reality for too many young people. In his inaugural professorial lecture at Durham University, Rob Coe assessed the performance of the English education system since 1994. Grade inflation and examination reform makes assessing this by comparing GCSE results in different years difficult.[2] So Coe gathered together all the data he could find on pupil attainment in a range of different international tests, allowing him to benchmark our pupils against those of a similar age in other countries. He also considered several studies which have carefully compared pupil standards over decades in English, maths and science.[3] His conclusion was bleak: "Standards have not risen; teaching has not improved."

Other metrics tell a similar story. Each year around 17 per cent of pupils leave school functionally illiterate[4], twelve years of compulsory education having got them almost nowhere. The gap in attainment between pupils who just make it into the top quarter of richest families (the 75th percentile), and those who just make into the third quarter of richest families (the 25th percentile) has remained high and broadly stable since the 1950s.[5] Standards have proven stubbornly resistant to change and inequalities have not closed.

This is not for lack of trying. Ministers have implemented any number of measures to try and improve failing schools. Kenneth Baker's Education Reform Act of 1988 introduced school choice for parents, which proponents hoped would put pressure on weaker schools to improve. In the nineties, leagues tables and Ofsted inspections were introduced to increase the pressure further still. New Labour initiatives such as Beacon Schools, the London Challenge and Specialist Leaders of Education sought to help weaker schools learn from others. Reductions in class sizes gave teachers more time with each pupil and armies of teaching assistants were drafted in to support the work of teachers in the classroom. These policies necessitated an increase in spending during the Labour government from 4.5 per cent of GDP when they took power, to 6.2 per cent of GDP when they lost it.[6] Labour also unleashed a tidal wave of capital investment in the form of the Building Schools for the Future programme, totalling £55bn over thirteen years.[7] A panoply of new types of schools have also been introduced: specialist schools, academy schools, free schools, studio schools. The Coalition government gave schools £2.5bn extra to help support their poorest pupils. And yet, Professor Coe, himself a former teacher, was forced to conclude that standards have not risen. To be clear, good things have happened and some notable bright spots have emerged. Overall, however, students are no better off.

How can so much money and effort have achieved so little? The answer to this apparently baffling question is remarkably simple. Policymakers have been looking in the wrong place.

Ministers are largely judged by their announcements: the white papers, parliamentary statements and press releases by which they communicate their reform plans. The general public, of course, consume these announcements in shortened clips on the evening news, or while flicking through the newspaper over breakfast. This creates a bias towards policies which are easy to describe in pithy, concrete language. Class sizes make for good announcements, because everyone knows what you are talking about and a pledge to cut them can be conveyed in a single sentence. A programme to replace old school buildings with modern facilities is even better, since the minister can also visit the school for a photo opportunity when it is reopened. Anything that involves spending more money on education has the air of a serious commitment. New school types are harder to communicate but tend to go down well since they appear to signal a clear break with whatever went before – a new way of doing things. Policy therefore tends toward the concrete and the intuitive.

Unfortunately – tragically, even – research has consistently shown that these policies have little effect on pupil learning. A recent evaluation of the Building Schools for the Future policy found it had no impact whatsoever on pupil progress.[8] School choice has a small effect, at best.[9] And even the most optimistic findings on class size suggests that it has only a very small impact, and at high cost.[10] Spending more money on education, without direction, is perhaps least effective of all.[11] Worse still, many of the policies we have been pursuing, such as school collaboration, are at present little more than guesswork, with little or no supporting evidence[12] – what Professor John Van Reenen from the Massachusetts Institute of Technology calls 'policy witchcraft'.[13]

Thankfully, however, there is one thing which does have an impact: teacher quality. Research consistently shows that the quality of instruction, which in turn depends upon the knowledge, skills and dispositions of teachers, is a powerful determinant of pupil learning.[14] Indeed, as Eric Hanushek from Stanford University puts it: "No other attribute of schools comes close." Moving a child from an average to a top teacher's class means they will learn in six months what would otherwise have taken twelve.[15] Moreover, good teachers seem to have a disproportionately strong impact on pupils from disadvantaged homes. Good teachers therefore also help to close the gap in attainment.[16] The beneficial effects of good teachers also stretch far beyond the examination hall. Raj Chetty, one of the most influential economists in the world, has calculated that moving a child from a poor quality (bottom 5 per cent) teacher to an average quality teacher increases their lifetime earnings by a quarter of a million dollars.[17] If improving the quality of education is the public policy holy grail, teachers are the ones who will find it for us.

For our children to thrive as adults then, our teachers need to thrive in the classroom. For all those involved in education, from the Secretary of State down to the parent-teacher association, there should be no greater priority than nurturing and retaining brilliant teachers. We should be offering them the best possible training, supporting them in any way we can and systematically removing any burdens which stand in the way of their success.

Precisely the opposite is the case. Improving the quality of our teaching workforce has rarely, if ever, been a genuine priority for government. Announcing a policy to improve teaching quality is neither concrete nor intuitive. Indeed, all too often the zeal with which policymakers have pursued other reforms has only served to make life harder for teachers. Box ticking demands – real or imagined – from the school inspectorate, ceaseless curriculum reform, disruptive top-down reorganisations, and an audit culture that requires teachers to document their every move have caused a huge increase in administrative workload and a drop in morale. Instead of rolling out the red carpet for our teachers we have been pulling it from under their feet. *This is the first sense in which we face a teacher gap: the disparity between what we know about the importance of teachers, and how we treat them.*

One of us, Sam, has been fixated with the potential of education from the age of sixteen. He thought about training as a teacher after university, and has since taught economics at A Level and Undergraduate level, but has narrowly escaped teaching in schools. Several of his friends and family did decide to train as teachers, however. Sam watched a whole cohort of them begin their training full of optimism and idealism, only to become steadily more exhausted and demoralised by the job. While his own managers showed a keen interest in his development and growth, the young teachers he knew seemed only to have complaints about the way they were treated by their schools. He began to wonder how – given everything we know about the importance of good teaching – we could be treating them so badly. As he saw more and more of his teacher friends move abroad to teach in international schools, move to private schools, or quit the profession altogether, his curiosity and frustration got the better of him. So four years ago he began work on a PhD to see what the data could tell us about what was going on.

Our failure to give teachers the support they need to thrive in the classroom has a predictable consequence: they leave it. The brutal asymmetry between the pressures we place on our teachers and the support we give them has led to an epidemic of burnout in the classroom and an exodus from the profession, far in excess of what we see in other European countries.[18,19] Perhaps most shockingly, around 40 per cent of those who decide to spend several thousand pounds and two years of their life to train as teachers are no longer working in publicly funded schools five years later. This is an unforgivable waste of human potential, taxpayers' money (we spend £700m a year training teachers) and of the transformative potential of good teaching.[20] This failure to retain early-career teachers forces the government to raise their target for recruiting teachers each year. But each year we miss the target by a larger margin: a 1 per cent deficit in 2013; a 5 per cent deficit in 2014; a 9 per cent deficit in 2015. *This is the second sense in which there is a teacher gap: the difference between the number of teachers we need, and the number we have.*

One of us, Becky, has personal experience of this. She worked in an investment bank after graduating to pay off student debts and learn how the economy really works (something an economics degree doesn't teach you). However, it was never her intention to stay in a job with so little moral purpose, so in 2002 she quit to train as a teacher. While the job was everything she had hoped it would be, in the sense that it was meaningful and watching pupils learn was rewarding, she also felt ill-prepared by her training. In her first teaching job, it quickly became clear there was no instruction available as to how to get better as a teacher. Indeed, it was not clear that anyone much cared if she did. There was precious little mentoring available. Her school just expected her to plod away year-after-year, learning (or not) through trial and error. It was because of this that, despite being hard work, teaching never really felt like a challenge;

just frustrating. So, Becky left the classroom to do a PhD in the economics of education, and fourteen years later she is still crunching data and conducting research to try to better understand pupils, teachers and education policy.

Professor Coe's analysis suggests that Becky's experience is likely to be widespread. If teachers are the most important influence on a child's progress at school, but progress has stalled, we need to look at what is happening in the teaching profession. To be very clear, there are literally thousands of brilliant teachers in England. We have been lucky enough to meet many of them while writing this book. However, if we are to eliminate illiteracy, raise attainment across the country and create a richer, happier and healthier nation, we need to see a sustained, widespread increase in the quality of teaching. *This is the third and most important sense of the teacher gap: the difference between the quality of teachers we currently have, and the quality of teachers we want.*

In a way, it is not surprising that we have ended up in this mess. Much educational research is not aimed at improving the quality of classroom practice, either directly or indirectly. And those studies that do have this goal in mind are often descriptive or advocate change without the scientific approach necessary to provide strong insights that can help school leaders and policymakers improve teaching and learning. In the absence of good evidence, we have been flying blind or, at best, feeling our way forward. Fortunately, the last decade has seen an explosion of rigorous research on teachers. This has been catalysed by the release of large government datasets in both the UK and the US containing detailed information on every aspect of teachers and their careers, as well as increased funding for rigorous experiments. This in turn has attracted a new generation of researchers committed to a more scientific approach. Their work has given us a far better understanding of why people become teachers, how they get better at their jobs, how to hire and retain the best teachers, and why so many of them leave. The findings are now piling up, providing rich insights for school leaders and policymakers in how to help all teachers improve their practice.

But the evidence they have produced is not always easy to interpret. The findings are often hidden behind academic pay walls and expressed in precise statistical terminology which is inaccessible to those without specialist training. Some of the challenges involved in utilising this research also stem from the age-old disciplinary divides in the social sciences. Our tradition, economics, excels in isolating the impact of one policy or phenomenon from the contextual noise in the data, but is less good at understanding *why* teachers, policymakers and children act the way they do. We have therefore been drawn to well-validated theories from psychology to organise and explain what we know from the economics research. Grounding what we know about teachers in basic human psychology also allows us to extrapolate more confidently from empirical research undertaken in other school systems, and develop a set of proposals which are more likely to address teachers' fundamental needs and motivations. This book fuses findings across these disciplines, as well as insights from sociology and cognitive science, to develop an evidence-based plan for closing the teacher gap.

Our thinking can be summarised simply enough: we need to give teachers a career worth having. Achieving this, however, is altogether more complicated. Throughout this book we will hear from teachers and ex-teachers who have given their all to teaching but have struggled to succeed in the classroom. Listening to their stories, and the way in which they have been treated, it is hard not to conclude that they have been set up to fail. But we will also hear from teachers who have benefited from the support necessary to flourish and develop into masters of their craft. Their stories help illustrate what the research tells us about how the profession needs to be reformed if we are to ensure that all teachers can succeed. This will require far reaching reform of the way that teachers are trained, recruited, deployed, developed and rewarded. Some of our recommendations are directed at policymakers, but a great deal of what we say is aimed at school leaders and teachers themselves. Some will require radical reform, but much of it will be about sustained marginal improvements. The constant that runs throughout what we say is our focus on what matters most to children in schools, the point of greatest leverage: the teacher gap.

CHAPTER TWO

Teacher expertise
Learning to cha-cha on a ship full of mouldy fruit

Imagine that, the day after qualification, a junior doctor was expected to manage the same caseload as a consultant doctor and deal with the same range of cases, from the quotidian and mundane to the rare and complex. They were never able to ask for assistance from a more experienced colleague during a consultation or an operation, having to wait until a patient was discharged before getting a second opinion. Indeed, imagine our fresh-faced junior doctor had never learnt anatomy and therefore could only partially and sketchily describe to their superiors the problems they had encountered in the previous lesson. Worse, when they observed their consultant treating patients effectively and tried the same techniques themselves, they often just didn't have the same effect. And imagine if the minute after they qualified, they were given little or no further academic training or examinations and could quite feasibly go through their whole career without updating their knowledge once.

Clearly this would be an absurd way to train a doctor. Yet it is precisely the environment in which we expect teachers to train. They are often expected to develop a career's-worth of lesson plans during their first year on the job, teach the same number of classes as colleagues with decades more experience, work in near-isolation in their individual classrooms, and teach a variety of pupils, many of whom behave and respond to stimuli in ways that are difficult to categorise or predict. And many go a whole career without any significant refreshers or updates to the evidence base underpinning their practice.

This comparison helps highlight some of the strange features of teacher training and we will return to it at several points in this chapter. It is not, however, meant to imply that teachers should simply become *more like doctors*. Quite the opposite, in fact. Understanding how we might better train and retain teachers requires us to take a careful look at the specifics of what teaching expertise is and where it comes from. Neither is the argument set out in this chapter meant to imply that the medical profession is always good at transferring expertise. Matthew Syed has exposed the way in which the medical profession often fails to learn from errors, an issue we will discuss in Chapter 6.[21] Rather, we employ the comparison to bring into sharp relief the assumptions we have made for so long about how a teaching career should work. This chapter sets out some of the most important findings from the frontier of teacher research in order to begin breaking down some of these assumptions. In doing so, it provides an important foundation for the rest of the book. In particular, this evidence is essential for making sense of the stories we will hear from teachers in later chapters. So, how does somebody get good at teaching?

Expertise is gained from experience. Quickly at first, then more slowly

Most of us assume that we get better at our job as we accumulate experience. The idea of a *learning curve* helps express the idea that, over time, our skills and capabilities follow an upward trajectory. Until fairly recently, it was only possible to plot learning curves for simple tasks: how many free-throws out of a hundred a basketball player could score; or how long it would take for a typist to correctly punch out 100 words. These could be measured easily and graphed to show how we learn from experience: a steady increase in the number of free-throws scored; or the number of accurate keystrokes per minute. Researchers diligently went about quantifying the rates and plotting the patterns by which humans acquired skills.

Teaching expertise, by contrast, was seen by educational researchers as too difficult to quantify. Pupil learning is multi-faceted, tricky to measure and influenced by too great a range of factors beyond the teacher's control. But then two things happened. First, governments began to administer regular, standardised exams, which provided systematic measurements of progress for each child (albeit restricted to the type of learning which can be measured in exams). This made the fruits of a teacher's labour partially visible. Second, the results were recorded in massive datasets including detailed information about the pupil's family background. This enabled researchers to peel away the many other factors, beyond the pupil's teacher, which affected their attainment in exams. The best researchers, using the best datasets, are now able to isolate teachers' effects on pupil learning and plot the rate at which this increases over time. (The box at the end of the chapter explains the methods used in more detail.)

The shape of the learning curve for each individual teacher is unique, with slightly different starting points and growth rates at each stage of their career. When we look across data on thousands of teachers, however, a clear pattern emerges. Figure 2.1 shows a learning curve for the average teacher plotted by researchers from Brown University. The horizontal axis shows a teacher's number of years of experience on the job and the vertical axis shows how this translates into increased pupil attainment. The first thing to notice is that teachers face a very steep learning curve after qualification. Unlike junior doctors, who spend their first years on the job conducting simple diagnostic tests and collecting information for more senior doctors to use in decision making, teachers are expected to make more or less all the decisions relating to the education of their pupils straight away. Indeed in some schools, newly-qualified teachers are banned from using any lesson plans or resources developed by other teachers, meaning they have to develop all their lesson plans during their first year on the job. We will meet one such teacher, Luke, in Chapter 5. After two or three years, teacher learning curves become notably less steep, meaning that an additional year of

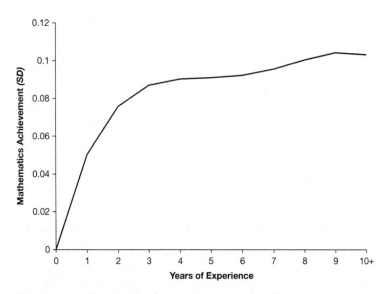

FIGURE 2.1 An illustration of typical returns to teaching experience

Adapted from Kraft, M.A. and Papay, J.P (2014)[22]

experience makes a smaller contribution to their expertise. Even so, the curve remains upward sloping across the first ten years of a teacher's career. Experience matters. Indeed, if we ranked one hundred teachers in terms of their expertise, with the most skilled teacher being put in position one, and least skilled in position one hundred, a teacher who starts their career in 73rd position would typically move to 50th due to the expertise acquired over the first decade on the job. Time in the classroom is a powerful performance enhancer.

How does experience translate into expertise and why is it so important for becoming a good teacher? In order to understand this we need to look away from the statistics to understand the world from a practitioner's point of view. In the late nineties, the US Army was thinking hard about how it could improve the skills of its officers and commissioned Robert Sternberg, a psychologist from Yale University, to investigate how professionals develop expertise. The research resulted in a book bringing together academics and practitioners working in professions including law, medicine, the military and teaching and it provides rich insights about the links between experience and professional judgement. An important theme developed by the contributors – particularly Jim Minstrell, a former teacher – is that teaching is an "ill-structured problem."[23] To illustrate this point Minstrell gives the example of knowing how far to encourage students' questioning and discussion of an issue in a classroom discussion, while not allowing the conversation to wander too far off track. Minstrell argues that it is impossible to imagine a set of principles that could be specified – in a teaching textbook, for example – that could tell a teacher when to encourage more conversation and when to reign it in.

Teaching can be aptly described as an 'ill-structured problem' precisely because most decisions faced by teachers are too idiosyncratic to be categorised. Imagine trying to write down a set of rules by which a teacher could determine whether to give the discussion more time to develop, or to move along with the lesson. It would be very difficult, because the answer is so highly dependent on the context: the pupils involved, the material being studied, and the trajectory, length and character of the discussion up until that point. If a set of rules could be devised, it would likely be so long as to be unusable. Try contrasting this with medicine, where detailed protocols for diagnosing and treating patients are widely used and we are starting to reach the point where computers can do some of the work involved. Children's minds are gloriously diverse and groups of children interact in complex and unpredictable ways.

In the absence of many rules or categorisations, teachers are left to rely on their professional judgement or wisdom. Decisions about when and where to curtail a class discussion are taken without conscious effort or systematic consideration of hypotheses.[24] Teachers rely instead on a subtle process of pattern recognition, in which they draw analogies with their internal database of similar past experiences, all of which have been remembered on some level, though very few of which could be individually recalled. The critical thing is that this bank of past cases and analogies can only be acquired through experience. Fortunately, there are also a few ways to give teachers a leg up their learning curves.

Schools can help teachers to keep learning

Although many teachers' learning curves begin to level off after a few years, this isn't the case for everyone. The same researchers from Brown University (who, by the way, won a prestigious award for this research[25]) wanted to know what could be done to sustain teachers' upward trajectories. They took detailed data on staff collaboration, training and quality of leadership and ranked all schools in North Carolina on the basis of how supportive they are of their teachers (see Figure 2.2). The bottom line shows what happens for teachers working in schools three quarters of the way down the ranking: schools which do relatively little to help their staff. The learning curve for these teachers seems to flatten off after about three years in the job. This is a startling finding: most of us would expect to keep growing and learning thirty years into our career, not plateau after just three. The middle line shows the growth in expertise for teachers in the average school, which is noticeably higher. But the most exciting part of the chart is the top line, which is the learning curve for teachers in schools that just about make it into the top quarter of most supportive schools. They continue to see strong growth in expertise through the ten-year period studied, with a noticeably higher growth rate than those in mid-ranking schools between years three and nine. These differences really stack up over time. A teacher following the top learning curve, in a more supportive school, will have gained 38 per cent more expertise from the first ten years on the job than a teacher following the bottom learning curve, in a less supportive school. More supportive schools therefore make experience an even more powerful performance enhancer. (We will return to consider why so many teachers plateau so quickly in Chapter 6).

Not all experience is equally valuable, however. Research by Ben Ost, an economist from the University of Illinois, shows that if a teacher is able to teach the same content in multiple years then they progress further up their learning curve.[27] Indeed, Ost shows that a year of experience teaching a specific part of the course – collecting like terms in algebra, for example, is worth between a third and half as much again as an additional year of general experience in maths

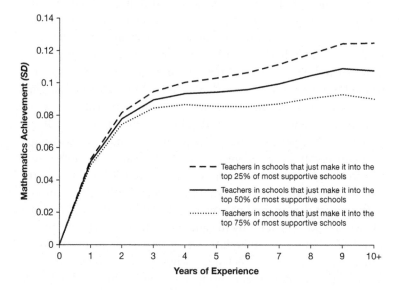

FIGURE 2.2 Predicted returns to teaching experience across schools with strong, average and weak working environments

Adapted from Kraft, M.A and Papay, J.P (2014)[26]

teaching. In a similar vein, recent research has shown that teachers are more effective when the types of students they are teaching are similar (e.g. in terms of their socio-economic background) to the types of students they taught when they trained.[28] The more relevant the cases stored in a teacher's mental database, the better the analogies they can draw to solve the ill-structured problems they encounter in future.

Interestingly, the effect also works in reverse. For every year it has been since a teacher delivers a specific part of the course, they lose around a third of their accumulated skills in teaching that subject. Just as teachers' mental databases can be expanded and strengthened, so the accumulated cases and comparisons stored there can be degraded and deleted. Providing teachers with some stability in the year groups and subject matter they teach therefore helps them get up, and stay up, their learning curves.[29]

Experience acquired while working with skilled colleagues is also a more powerful performance enhancer. Detailed data on teacher social networks has allowed researchers to track in minute detail the way in which teachers approach each other for advice and show how different techniques spread from one colleague to another by word of mouth. One team of researchers, led by Min Sun from Virginia Tech University, found that when a teacher's colleague received training on a new method of writing instruction, they gained 10 per cent as much expertise as the colleague who attended the training.[30] Economists call this a *spillover effect*. Two separate research teams, one from Stanford and one from Cornell, have tried to quantify the size of the spillover effect on pupil learning.[31] The best estimates we have suggest that approximately one fifth of the variation in teacher expertise is accounted for by the quality of their colleagues.[32] Strong working relationships therefore act as important pathways along which expertise can flow, helping teachers draw on the larger, more diverse archive of experience of their colleagues. Indeed, the Brown study shows that learning from peers is the single most important characteristic of schools that manage to sustain growth in teacher expertise.[33] Learning from peers provides a hand up the learning curve, shortcutting the time-consuming, trial-and-error process required for teachers to find their own way up the incline.

But as well as the familiar process of asking for advice, there is another, more specific reason why colleagues are such an important source of expertise for teachers. We have already discussed how much of what constitutes good teaching is difficult to pinpoint or codify in general rules or principles. There is nothing mysterious or mystical about this, it just means that professional judgment has to be used, and this generally has to be gained through experience. But it has a further implication, which is that expert teachers are not always able to articulate what they know in the form of simple advice. As Michael Polanyi puts it, they "know more than they can tell."[34] This makes observing skilled colleagues a potentially valuable source of learning, since it allows teachers to soak up some of the wisdom embedded in their colleagues' practice. This process takes time, since observing others can only provide suggestions and hints as to what is effective. But through being immersed in a community of skilled teachers, expertise can be transferred between teachers.[35] Learning from colleagues results from watching them, as well as listening to them.

The trouble is that teachers are often isolated in their classrooms (sometimes quite literally, as we will see when we hear Abi's story in the next chapter). Even teachers with well-established networks can sometimes struggle to know which of their colleagues has the expertise they need to draw on. Again, this stands in stark contrast to the medical profession, where there is a clear hierarchy of expertise organised within well-defined specialisms. Requests for advice can be passed up the food chain from graduate, to trainee, to registrar and eventually to the consultant. The hierarchies of expertise in schools are less obvious. This highlights the important role that middle and even senior leaders in schools can play in helping teachers share expertise. By knowing the specific development needs of different teachers, and which other staff are best placed to advise on or model good teaching, school leaders can act like telephone operators, making the connections through which expertise can be shared. Research consistently shows that, on a day-to-day basis, creating and sustaining the culture of collaborative, trusting relationships that allow this is the most powerful thing that school leaders can do to contribute to improved pupil progress.[36] Indeed, one recent experiment conducted in North Carolina suggests that after carefully assessing teachers' skills, just inviting those with complementary skills sets to talk to each other causes impressive gains in the expertise of the weaker teacher.[37]

Expertise is acquired in stages

We have already compared teaching and medicine on a number of fronts: the gradient of the learning curve; the ease with which problems can be defined and categorised; and the ease with which the expertise of others can be accessed. But perhaps the starkest contrast between the two professions is the way in which training is staged: medical training is gradual; teacher training is front-loaded.

When a junior doctor decides to specialise in surgery they follow a clear pathway, beginning with hospital shifts where they learn general skills like putting in cannulas or stitching up wounds. When these have been mastered, they will begin to spend more time on surgical wards. At first they will spend most of their time in theatre assisting on and observing more experienced surgeons at work and practising "closing" (stitching up) patients after surgery. Their first full operation might be a fairly straightforward appendectomy, under the careful instruction and supervision of a more experienced surgeon. By this point they can probably close the patient without a second thought, allowing them to focus their full attention on the novel, more sophisticated elements of the new procedure. Once they have mastered the components of these simpler procedures, they will grow their repertoire of general surgical procedures. Then, once these have been mastered they will begin to specialise in rare and more complex procedures, at each stage working under the supervision of a more experienced surgeon. Their training is gradual and sequential.[38]

Teacher training, by contrast, is almost entirely front-loaded. There are a wide variety of training routes for secondary teachers in the UK,[39] but all share this basic feature: 100 per cent of the formal training and certification comes in the first two years of a teacher's career. This means that all of their instruction in different teaching techniques, from the basics such as classroom management, through to advanced skills, such as assessment design, are delivered at once, prior to receiving Qualified Teacher Status. Inset days and observations or mentoring are used to deliver additional advice, but this is not comparable to the staged, supervised and examined sequence that clearly scaffolds progression through a medical career. After a teacher qualifies there are no requirements to gain further qualifications or progress through any professional stages. Unfortunately, this radically front-loaded training model flies in the face of what we know about the way in which people climb the learning curve.

Learning the skills of teaching, or any other profession for that matter, requires deliberate practice.[40] Practice allows trainee surgeons to move from being a novice, at which point they rely on an effortful, conscious process of working through each procedure step-by-step, through to becoming more expert, by which time they understand the task in a holistic way and are able to complete it in a more automatic, flexible manner. David Berliner gives the analogy of learning to cha-cha dance. At first, a student learns the steps (one, two, one-two-three) and can think about little else, staring down at their feet while they attempt to move each one in the right direction, in the correct order.[41] After several weeks of practice paying close attention to the footwork, however, they will think not of the different steps, only of doing the cha-cha. They can then concentrate on embellishing the basic footwork with more stylish upper body movements, responding to the specifics of the music and of their partner. In everyday parlance, we would say that an expert cha-cha dancer can perform the steps 'with their eyes closed'. This is because, following a long period of conscious, effortful practice, the steps have been stored deep in long-term memory.[42,43] This is what frees up bandwidth in their scarce working memory to focus on acquiring the next layer of skill. Teachers are no different to cha-cha dancers or junior doctors. Their ascent up the learning curve also has to be done step by step, with each new skill, alongside the instruction and feedback necessary to learn it, acquired one after another.[44] Trying to climb the curve too quickly will overload short-term memory causing teachers to slip and lose their footing.[45] Teaching expertise, like other expertise, must be acquired in stages.

Unfortunately, this is precisely the opposite of the approach taken by our front-loaded teacher training system, which provides minimal access to training after the first nine months. Most are just getting to grips with the basics of lesson planning and classroom management 18 months *after* they have completed their training. The idea that they can be simultaneously acquiring advanced skills is, to put it gently, unscientific. By the time teachers are ready to start integrating more advanced techniques into their repertoire they are often years away from their formal training and will likely have forgotten the content of those parts of the course. Indeed, they may have written them off as unworkable after struggling to combine them with other skills early on, before they had the necessary spare bandwidth in working memory to try and assimilate them.[46] Front-loaded teacher training is like preparing for a six-month sea voyage by stocking up the hold of the ship with fresh fruit. By the time the crew get around to eating their second week of supplies, it will all have gone off. Cramming training in advanced (or even intermediate) techniques into the first two years of a teacher's career is no less wasteful, or unwise. It is very likely one of the reasons that the average teacher learning curve begins to flatten off after around three years in the classroom. Only in the schools that provide sustained opportunities for training, practice and feedback – like those shown in the top line of Figure 2.1 – can teachers continue up their learning curve.

*   *   *

The battle to improve education for our children is largely a battle to help teachers up their learning curves. The good news, as we have tried to set out in this chapter, is that we now know quite a lot about how to help them make the climb. The best schools provide an environment where sustained teacher growth is possible, providing them with stable class assignments to help them reap the maximum rewards from experience and providing the opportunities and environment for them to learn from colleagues as they go, accelerating their ascent up the curve. The bad news is that many schools are doing the opposite and frontloaded teacher training remains universal. In Chapter 3 we will see how the system makes it near-impossible for many new teachers to become skilled. In Chapter 4 we will see how schools are able to get away with running a recruit–burnout–replace model of staffing in which novice teachers are replaced with yet more novice teachers. And in Chapter 5 we will see how policymakers and school leaders have undermined teachers' motivation to persist in the difficult, effortful climb up their learning curves. But as well as diagnosing the problems that the teaching profession faces, we will also set out what school leaders and policy-makers can do to provide teachers with the support, motivation and carefully sequenced training they need to keep climbing their learning curves long into their careers. In each chapter we will hear from real teachers who illustrate the problems faced by the profession and point the way towards solutions.

Things that schools can do without waiting for policymakers

- Where possible, provide teachers with stable, specialised teaching assignments. This will allow them to acquire skills faster. Science teachers in England often teach three subjects, for example, but would likely be more effective if they specialised. This is particularly important for new teachers.

- Where you have teachers who need to improve, either because they are inexperienced or otherwise, who will they be learning from? Where weaknesses are widespread in a given department, construct cross-departmental collaborative or mentoring arrangements to help transfer expertise.[52]

- Measure the quality of the working environment in your school each year. This can be done using the short survey used by the *Brown* researchers, which is included in the annex of their free-to-access paper.[53] Be sure to make it anonymous, however, and emphasise that it is not being used for performance management purposes. Identify the areas in which your school is weak and target improvements in this area the following year. Improving the quality of the working environment should help teachers in your school develop expertise faster.

- School leaders can make teaching in their school or department less of an 'ill-structured problem' for new teachers by standardising certain routines, for example around discipline. This narrows the number of choices teachers must make, freeing them up to focus on developing new skills.

How do we know that some teachers are more effective than others?

Most of us can think back to our time at school and name specific teachers from whom we learned a lot and others from whom we learned not so much. We can remember teachers who were rarely even in the classroom; others who couldn't control the class to begin the process of instruction each lesson; others where we had glorious fun in their lessons, but felt ill-prepared for the GCSE exam at the end of the two years; and others on whose every word we hung. But moving beyond these anecdotes to establish that there is variation in the quality of teachers using hard data is challenging.

First of all, you need good measures of pupil learning. Fortunately, high-stakes, standardised, externally-marked exams have generated a lot of good data on this in recent years. Moreover, several US states have introduced *annual* standardised tests that measure what children know when they enter a teacher's class and what they know when they leave, isolating the progress achieved while with an individual teacher. Of course, some pupils make apparent learning gains that are not actually real – there can be marking errors or students get lucky on the questions asked that day. Indeed, looking at teacher value-added for a single class in a single year has been shown to be systematically unreliable.[47] Fortunately, however, the large datasets now available to study these questions mean that this sort of random noise tends to get averaged out over very many observations.

But even having access to a lot of good data is not enough to isolate the contribution of individual teachers. Factors such as the curriculum and school-specific discipline policies all affect learning gains, vary over time and across classrooms, and are partly outside the control of individual teachers. This creates a risk that we misattribute pupil progress (or lack thereof) to a specific teacher, when it is really due to incidental things beyond their control. To tackle this issue, economists compare teachers working in the same schools at the same time. These teachers face the same discipline problems, for example, which enables them to hold such factors constant.[48] Studies using these techniques consistently find differences in teacher quality. Another way of trying to ensure that we are not fooled by contextual noise in the data is to look at whether teachers who are effective in one school remain effective in another school. Chetty, Friedman and Rockoff show that this is indeed true: overall attainment in a school deteriorates when measurably effective teachers leave the school and overall attainment increases when a measurably effective teacher joins a school.[49]

Even then, a sceptic might reply that perhaps good teachers gravitate towards improving schools and bad teachers are forced to resort to jobs in schools on their way down. However, a large study funded by the Bill and Melinda Gates Foundation randomly assigned teachers to classrooms and compared their effectiveness across years. It found that teacher effectiveness is correlated from one year to the next: teachers who appeared effective in one year tended to be effective the next year, and vice versa.[50] Because teachers were randomly assigned to classrooms in each year, we can be confident that this result is not driven by pupil intake, school policies, teachers applying for different types of jobs, and so on.

Even still, an arch-sceptic might object that perhaps the teachers that see the best test score gains among their pupils are just better at teaching to the test but do not create more genuine learning than their colleagues. However, in an important final piece of the jigsaw, Raj Chetty and colleagues show that being taught by an effective teacher improves a student's long-run economic outcomes (income) and social success as an adult, suggesting that these teachers really are making a difference to pupils' learning, rather than just their test scores.[51]

CHAPTER THREE

Teacher retention
Why Abi and James now work in the City

I have arranged to meet Abi and James in a coffee shop on London's Chancery Lane. Corporate types hover in front of the till, tapping their feet impatiently as they wait for the baristas to push cardboard cups across the counter. Outside, crowds of people are striding purposefully back to their offices with paper bags containing their lunch: lawyers, consultants, developers, media types. Amazon and Skype are headquartered here and Goldman Sachs are building their new office nearby. Three years ago Abi and James had just enrolled at the most prestigious teacher training institute in the UK. Abi had quit her job with a healthcare regulator in order to retrain as a teacher. Both of them had invested a year of their life and £9,000 of their own money on getting qualified. And both of them had committed themselves, psychologically, to a career in the classroom. Now both work for a nearby legal firm. I was here to try and understand what had happened in between. How had two seemingly professional and engaging graduates gone from there, to dropping out of teaching altogether, in just a couple of years?

I blow on my coffee as they talk me through their stories. James had placements in secondary schools in Dagenham and Newham, teaching business and economics. Abi worked in primary schools in Westminster and Clerkenwell. Both found it easy to get full time teaching positions after leaving university and both had quit by the end of their first year on the job. Their story is far from unusual. Indeed, Abi is quick to point out that 9 of the 18 teachers in her teacher training group had already left the profession. James momentarily looks surprised by this, before pausing for a moment to think about his own cohort and then nodding in recognition. A study by the National Audit Office shows how teachers leave at every stage of the process: around one in ten of those who enter training each year fail to qualify, a further tenth enter alternative professions after qualification[54] and half as many again decide to teach in private schools.[55] This leaves around three quarters of the original cohort to enter classrooms in publicly funded schools. But by the end of the first year in the classroom only two-thirds of the original cohort are left.[56] Abi and James are just two more members of this 'missing third'.

How worried should we be about these teachers who never make it? Plenty of the young graduates who get their first jobs in the law firms, advertising agencies and banks around Chancery Lane quickly realise they have made a mistake and then change careers. In any case, the annual School Workforce Census for England shows that more teachers join the profession than leave in any given year: the total number of teachers is going up, not down.[57] But the missing third of teachers who left during their training or first year teaching matters for a number of reasons. First, as we saw in Chapter 2, teachers develop expertise at a rapid rate during their first two years on the job. This means that, even if we can replace the teachers who leave after their first year, we will be replacing them with another set of inexperienced teachers who are yet to acquire even basic skills. In effect, there are an additional 4,589 classrooms in England manned by less experienced teachers as a result of these teachers leaving. And retention is getting steadily worse with each new cohort of trainees.[58]

Second, because the number of pupils is rising quickly, simply replacing the teachers that leave is no longer sufficient.[59] The Department for Education (DfE) uses a sophisticated model to estimate the number of new teachers required each year. As the pupil population has begun to grow these targets have been missed by increasing amounts: a 1 per cent deficit in 2012/13; a 5 per cent deficit in 2014; a 9 per cent deficit in 2015. The shortage for 2015 is equivalent to 3,201 teachers.[60] This is notably less than the 4,589 teachers who left during their first year on the job in 2011/12 suggesting that better early-career retention could go a long way towards closing the teacher gap.

Third, and this is not a point that should be underestimated, it is a real personal loss for the teachers who drop out. As the interview progresses, Abi and James begin to relax and open up about how the experience made them feel. In Abi's words, "Every morning I would get up and feel just so nervous, almost like I would want to vomit." James admitted that working seven days a week and "never being able to switch off" caused him difficulties sleeping. These examples may sound extreme but research consistently identifies teaching as being among the most stressful of professions.[61] The regret with which Abi and James looked back on the whole episode was palpable during the interview, not least the money they had each spent on training. Abi's voice wavered as she recalled her fear that by quitting she would be letting her parents down.

Fourth, and this is surely the most important reason, high levels of teacher turnover are bad for pupils. As well as the drain on management time and school resources, high turnover can cause serious disruption to pupil's learning. This is something with which James had personal experience.

> The teacher before me was loved by her class but she had to leave. When I came along there was this massive wall up because they thought, 'Oh this one is going to leave soon too.' That put a barrier up between me and the class.

Recent research from the US confirms that James's personal experience is a general problem: high teacher turnover damages pupil attainment.[62] Poorer pupils are both more likely to be in schools with high turnover and seem to suffer most from its effects.[63]

This loss of newly qualified teachers must be stemmed. But how? Early research on teacher turnover showed that teachers are much more likely to leave if they work in schools with lots of poor, low attaining kids. What's more, the teachers who move schools rather than leaving the profession altogether, generally find new teaching jobs in more affluent schools.[64] This finding has been replicated many times since, including in our own research using data from England.[65] James and Abi regularly referred to behavioural issues and "underlying social problems" as we discussed the challenges they faced in the classroom, shooting knowing, empathetic glances at each other when it came up. This is a somewhat depressing finding: if teachers are fleeing from difficult pupils, then the prospects of improving education in these schools are not good.

Thankfully, a recent reinterpretation of the research by Susan Johnson and colleagues at Harvard University is beginning to change the way we think about what drives teachers away. Johnson's research shows that, when researchers account for how much support schools give new teachers, the correlation between the type of pupils at the school and poor teacher retention melts away.[66] Put another way, it turns out that teachers are not fleeing poor pupils but are in fact fleeing schools in which they do not receive the right professional support. Schools with lots of poor pupils struggle to provide enough support, but where they do, retention is similar to that in affluent schools. Supportive working conditions are robustly predictive of retention for all teachers, but they seem to be particularly important for early-career teachers.[67] Quantitative research, including our own, consistently shows that the most important things for improving retention are the quality of leadership, opportunities for collaboration with colleagues, and appropriate teaching assignments and training.[68] Susan Johnson's own research, following a cohort of fifty trainees through their first few years in the profession, illustrates powerfully how these supportive working conditions help teachers to develop skills and acquire a 'sense of success' in the classroom.[69] Researchers working at Teach First in England conducted a similar study with their trainee teachers and reached similar conclusions: to survive the difficult first couple of years in the classroom, new teachers need a shoulder to cry on and a role model to learn from.[70]

It was clear that Abi had neither of these. She told me how her temporary classroom was located in the school car park, meaning she was physically separated from the rest of the school. During lunch break she was so busy with lesson planning and book marking that she struggled to find time to visit the staff room. Come Friday evening, it is traditional for NQTs to go to the local together for a pint or two. This may sound like the beginning of their weekend but it's actually an integral part of the working week, allowing them to swap stories from their week, exchange information about specific pupils, reassure each other that nobody is particularly good at teaching in the first year on the job, and generally decompress. It's a collective shoulder to cry on. But Abi was the only trainee at her small primary school and on Friday nights the other, older teachers went home to their families. Abi found herself drifting home to a pile of marking. "I found that so difficult," she admitted. "Really isolated, actually." Despite having many experienced colleagues, Abi also had nobody who acted as a role model for her. "I really respond well to feedback of any kind, positive or negative. But there was such an absence of that." She did get feedback from school leaders, but only at the end of the year, when they informed her that some of her students hadn't made enough progress. By that point she had already decided to quit teaching.

James's experience was more varied. He struggled in his first training placement. Our research surveying PGCE students in London shows that this is typical – measured levels of stress increase substantially once trainees are sent into schools.[71] His second placement was even tougher, with what he described as "severe behavioural issues." But the support he got was of a high standard. He was asked to identify weaknesses in his teaching and was given clear, focused advice on how to improve. "They would say, in order to achieve this, you need to do this and to focus on one thing at a time." It made all the difference. "Things just naturally progressed and by the end I did have control of the classroom, it was faster paced and more learning was happening." Crucially, this sense of progression changed his outlook and motivation. "I was very, very happy in that placement. I loved teaching. I thought I had finally turned the corner and could see myself with a career in teaching." He felt confident leaving his second placement to go into his NQT year. But then he moved to a school in Kent, and the story changed.

James was asked to teach accounting, a subject in which he had no training and no experience teaching, and his mentor was absent for several weeks during the first term. He did have a replacement mentor from another subject, but they were only able to give him generic advice.

> I was staying up all night teaching myself about double-entry book keeping. The students were fine in my business lessons, but they could work out I wasn't a specialist in the other subjects. They were just trying to catch me out.

In the end, he felt that so much time went into behavioural issues that he was never able to develop his teaching skills. Research shows that asking early career teachers to deliver multiple subjects, particularly those for which they have not been trained, is associated with worse retention.[72] James was no different.

To leave teaching after investing all that time and effort must have been a big decision. I asked Abi what finally made up her mind. She pauses before responding, "I never really saw any kind of improvement." When I pushed her on whether she had really not improved at all after a whole year of practice, she conceded that she must have, a bit. But with nobody giving her feedback of any kind, she was unable to recognise her own achievements. "As a new teacher, a trainee teacher, I never knew if I was doing the right thing. Nobody was feeding that back to me." Ultimately she lost confidence in her own abilities. "I felt completely inadequate. I think in order to do a good job you need to feel confident and I never did. So, I never felt that buzz which everybody talked about." It was becoming clear to me that Abi and James's experience as early-career teachers were inimical to developing the 'sense of success' that Johnson's research suggests is so important for early career teachers (we will return to this idea in Chapter 5).

At the same time, there were plenty of things Abi hated about the job. Foremost among these was the paperwork around lesson planning. As she put it, "Why do I have to write it down in such detail when it's in my head. It's such a waste of time." Abi's school required all teachers to fill out what she described as a "huge planning template with hundreds of different boxes." This had to be filled in for every lesson including a series of check boxes to ensure that each lesson included elements to address the needs of "audio", "visual" and "kinaesthetic" learners, as well as questions differentiated for the five different ability groups in her class. Abi had to have a copy of every lesson plan on the computer system with two more copies printed off for the files of the leadership team. Often this involved coming in early on a Monday morning in order to do the necessary filing. "It was horrendous and totally unnecessary, because nobody read it, not even the leadership team." Three evenings a week would also be taken up with meetings, often over trivial issues like which colour pen the school should use for marking. "I found that really strange about teaching . . . It wasn't an efficient system at all." James nodded his agreement: "You would just be thinking, *get on with it*, I need to get home to this stack of marking." This is a common complaint across the profession, and one we'll return to in Chapter 7.

Why did James and Abi quit so quickly? After all, young professionals frequently put in long hours at work and have to comply with all sorts of demands from management. Psychologists have developed a powerful framework which explains people's commitment and motivation at work: the Job Demands Resources model (JDR).[73] As the name suggests it has two components. Demands are things that require sustained effort and are perceived by the individual as a hindrance such as conflict, office politics and red tape.[74] Demands drain people's energy and if they are too intense can result in exhaustion, disengagement and ultimately burnout. On the other side of the ledger are resources. This is anything that helps people achieve their goals such as training, feedback and social support. These increased resources help people succeed at work by promoting vigorous engagement and enabling a problem solving approach to difficulties. The theory has been tested repeatedly by researchers and a review carried out by academics from the Universities of Florida and California shows that the model accurately explains why people become disengaged from their work across a whole range of professions, including teaching.[75]

The model fits Abi and James's story neatly. The demands placed on them were very great and both saw the lesson planning, meetings and marking as hindrances, preventing them from getting on with their job. At the same time, they had very few resources to draw on in terms of support from colleagues or mentors. The effect this had on Abi and James is also consistent with the JDR model, which predicts that when job demands exceed job resources this drains people's energy and motivation, eventually leading to a state of burnout in which they become emotionally exhausted and detached from their work. Eventually this disengagement culminates in teachers leaving their job.[76] Abi describes how, after a few months, she:

> hated going into the building itself. I hated the working environment. I felt overwhelmed with work. I made my decision to leave in December and from January to July I had a calendar which I literally used to tick off the days . . . I refused to put up with how it made me feel any longer.

But the JDR model is also a reminder that it doesn't have to be like this. Newly qualified teachers will be exhausted no matter what. Teaching a class full of children is *hard*. But with the right support they can engage constructively with the challenges of learning to teach, secure in the knowledge that their colleagues will help them get through it. As Toby Salt, former Chief Executive of the Ormiston Academies Trust, puts it: "It is the support that makes the challenge bearable, inspiring rather than undermining."[77] With the right balance of demands and resources, however, teachers will survive long enough to start developing some real skill. Before long the feedback they receive will begin to reflect this improvement and their confidence will grow. They will develop a strong voice, develop fluent classroom management and in due course will be able to incorporate more sophisticated methods into their teaching, perhaps even a bit of flair. And after two or three years in the classroom the research shows they will have scaled the steepest bit of the learning curve and become substantially more effective.[78] If they can get to this point, then the data shows that very few of them will leave.[79] They will have secured that all important 'sense of success'. But too many teachers never make it.

Every time a school treats a new teacher like Abi or James were treated, they are running the risk of pushing a teacher out of the profession. The recruitment process required to replace them will be expensive and disruptive for the school and if they replace them with another newly qualified teacher then another class in their school will spend another year being taught by a novice teacher. As a country, it is in our interest to avoid this happening. It is certainly in the pupils' interest. But the fact that around 5,000 new teachers are leaving each year suggests that schools don't seem to get it. Why? Research by Professor Shirley Andrews and colleagues provides one intriguing answer.[80] They surveyed early-career teachers in the State of Georgia and asked them whether they received twelve different types of support, such as having a mentor, or having the chance to plan lessons with other more experienced teachers. They then asked the same questions to school leaders. Interestingly, they found that school leaders were much more likely to believe that they offered support than early-career teachers were to think that they received it. For example, 90 per cent of school leaders reported that their beginning teachers were given constructive, non-evaluative feedback, while only 34 per cent of teachers agreed. Similarly, 82 per cent of school leaders reported providing tailored professional development for beginning teachers, while only 58 per cent of beginning teachers reported receiving this. It appears then, that school leaders think they are being more supportive than they actually are. In Chapter 4, we will see another reason that schools fail to provide the necessary support that is altogether more sinister.

Fortunately, research also provides a number of useful insights about how school leaders can better support new teachers. For Abi and James, however, it is already too late. My interview with them has flown by and James is forced to point out that his lunch break is already over. I push open the door of the café and the sound of traffic rushes in from the street outside. As Abi steps out she tells me excitedly that she is starting her "dream job" next week at the Independent Press Standards Organisation, set up in the wake of the phone hacking scandal. She gestures down a side road to where their offices are located. Teaching was Abi and James's dream once, but having heard their stories I am hardly surprised that they have given up on it, especially when they can choose between any number of well-paid positions with the big graduate employers. I tell them I hope it hasn't been too depressing to retell their stories. They both laugh, but before we go our separate ways Abi's expression becomes more serious. "It's such a shame," she says, "because I still think it could be such a fantastic job."

* * *

One hundred and twenty miles north of Holborn is the town of Bournville, in the suburbs of Birmingham. When the town's train station was first opened in 1876 it served nothing more than a few scattered houses in the countryside south of the city. But in 1879, two enterprising brothers, George and Richard, spotted the potential of the area for relocating their business. It had enough open space for them to build a large new factory, away from the crowded city centre; the canals allowed them to get milk delivered by barge from surrounding farms; and the railways allowed them to take deliveries of cocoa from ports on the south coast. But the location also presented them with a challenge: how would they attract and retain the workers necessary to staff their chocolate factory when it was located so far from the city centre?

Their answer, part hard-headed pragmatism and part high-minded idealism, was to build the model village of Bournville, which would provide a lifestyle so attractive that they would have no problem finding staff. The wide roads are lined with spacious family homes: red brick, exposed beams and large, well-kept front gardens. The Cadburys were keen on supporting the wellbeing of their staff. There is the Bournville bowls green, the Bournville boating lake, the Bournville cricket pitch and the Bournville playing fields, all of which were free to use for employees and their families. Although their Quakerism meant they did not allow any pubs in the village, the Cadbury brothers also established a number of social institutions to help bring the community together. They pioneered the use of workers' committees to give employees more influence at work and they established an evening school to allow employees to further their education. When it became clear that enthusiastic staff were getting tired from combining a day at work with an evening of lectures, the company allowed them time off from work to attend classes during the day. It is difficult to underestimate the contrast between life in Bournville and the conditions endured by the working classes in the dirty, cramped Victorian inner city of the time. The Cadburys transformed the working conditions of their employees.

I am in Birmingham to hear about another pioneering institution which is trying to do the same for teachers. Five minutes' walk from the edge of Bournville is the University of Birmingham School. The building stands out in an otherwise historic area of the city: modern, angular and purposeful. It was established in 2014 and, along with the University of Cambridge Primary School, it is one of only two so-called University Training Schools in the country.

Frances Child, the Vice Principal, greets me at reception with a wide smile and leads me into the huge, three story, sunlit atrium around which all the classrooms are organised. On the way she stops to pick up a crisp packet from the otherwise spotless floor. "I am obsessed with picking up litter," she confides. We settle ourselves in an empty classroom on the third floor and Frances tells me about the unique collaboration they have with Birmingham University, where she is also the Head of the Department of Teacher Education. She is positively overflowing with ideas, not least for how they can treat early-career teachers better. "I'm very, very clear that we need teachers who stay," she tells me early on in our discussion. There are currently twelve NQTs working at the school and the school's approach to developing, assigning and retaining them is a case study in the deft application of the Job Demands Resources model. Frances repeatedly describes it as a "careful introduction to teaching" in which the demands placed on new teachers are consciously controlled. "It is not about throwing people into anything," she explains. They do their very best to limit the amount of unnecessary, draining administrative tasks. "I'm not very interested in marking, not very interested in lots of things being written down, we're pretty cool about data. We don't want people spending hours on their books and our lesson observations are based around conversations," she informs me. "We think a lot about workload, it's a very high priority." I tell them about Abi being forced to write, copy and deposit a plan for every lesson at her school. Frances sighs, "Somebody needs to tell them to stop."

But even more impressive is the work that the school is doing to improve support. Like the Cadbury brothers, they recognise the brute fact that unless they make the job enjoyable they will never attract or retain the staff they need. Each of their NQTs is paired up with a Teaching Fellow who works with them on their overall development and professionalism. They are also assigned to a separate mentor who focuses on their pedagogy and subject knowledge, spending an hour a fortnight helping the teachers brush up on the specifics of their job, whether it be circle theorems or oil painting brush techniques. I can't help but think about how much James would have benefited from this sort of help when he was struggling to deliver lessons on accounting without any training or preparation. Frances is clear that it's the quality of training provided that matters. She contrasts the coaching given at her school with what she has seen on other NQT programmes, where on one occasion the sum total of advice given to a trainee in one session was a reminder to charge the video camera for the upcoming lesson!

As well as this support with the technical aspects of the job, Frances and her team clearly understand the importance of supportive networks. The last day of every half term is given over to training. The pupils do not come in to school and staff use the time to work together on preparing resources for lessons, do yoga or go running together. And every week during term the teachers do five hours of "enrichment" with pupils: chess, debating, rugby, cycling, knitting or whatever the teachers and pupils want to do together. Besides introducing the pupils to new ideas and hobbies, this is all designed to build relationships between teachers from different departments and allow the teachers to bond with the pupils. It would have been just the right excuse for Abi to get out of her carpark classroom and bond with her colleagues. I admit doing a double take at the point that Frances mentioned compulsory knitting. How on earth could it be worth keeping overworked teachers in school for another hour to make scarfs? I must have unwittingly raised an eyebrow because Frances pauses, and then reinforces the point, "Oh yes, we do a lot of knitting here."

Perhaps sensing my scepticism, she takes me to meet two of their NQTs, Lindsey (art) and Natasha (biology). I ask them if the school is different to those where they did their PGCE placements. "The culture is very different here," Lindsey tells me. "You don't shut yourself in your classroom at break. And the data stuff at my old school, jumping through hoops, was a real waste of my time." She adds that "having lots of other NQTs here is really good, because you don't have to pretend you know everything. It allows me to be honest." Natasha concurs, "I'm enjoying it more here. I like that one minute you can be teaching and the next you are cooking with students and some of the other teachers. It changes your relationship with them." Frances beams: "It's those relationships that are super-important." Both Lindsey and Natasha admit that the job is demanding, but neither of them sound burned out. "When I got the job I wondered if I would be able to cope with the longer days," Natasha tells me. "But I haven't noticed it much." Early-career teachers here work just as hard as teachers anywhere else. The difference is that they spend far less time grappling with the burdensome, demoralising demands of form-filling and data collection and far more time doing what they set out to do: learning to teach. And they are supported through this with the resources they need to do the job: carefully crafted coaching and support networks. The number of hours they put in is not all that different to the average NQT. What is unusual is that their job and working conditions have been designed to ensure that the balance between the demands placed on them and resources available to them ensure they can acquire a sense of success and avoid burnout.[81]

At the end of that academic year I contacted Frances to thank her again for showing me around the school and catch up on how things were going. All twelve NQTs were still at the school and were planning to stay for the next academic year. That's a retention record the Cadbury brothers would have been proud of achieving in their model village. For Abi and James though, it's back to the City.

Things that schools can do without waiting for policymakers

- Your novice teachers are at greatest risk of disrupting your school and the education of the children by leaving at the end of the year. Put their needs first by minimising the demands you place on them. Allocate their timetable and rooms before everyone else. Give them stable, specialised teaching assignments in subjects they have studied at degree level. In a secondary school, see whether they can 'double-up' by teaching the same lessons twice to different classes each week. Give them a dedicated classroom, even if this means the Head of Department goes without!

- Consider the resources you are providing your novice teachers. The induction programme you run should reflect their needs as the academic year progresses, including ongoing support with developing basic skills. Ensure that the support provided to them is non-judgemental and entirely separate from performance management. If it's not, it may be interpreted as a demand rather than a resource.

- The most important support new teachers receive is from other teachers in the school. Each new teacher needs someone to learn from. It is critical that mentors act as genuine role models, rather than just going through the motions and doing the paperwork.

- New teachers also need a shoulder to cry on. It might not be possible for a headteacher to plan who this should be, but they can put channels in place to encourage staff to step up to this role. Ask those teachers who are just a few years ahead of the new teachers to act as emotional support.

CHAPTER FOUR

Teacher hiring
Sausages and lemons

Ellen was a straight-A student at school and would, by her own admission, print off the mark schemes at the beginning of a new school year so as to make sure she would deliver on everything that was asked of her. A personable and lively drama student, she had originally intended to work in prisons, but a short drama placement in a primary school got her hooked on teaching. She beams across the table at me as she recalls her experience as a trainee. Unlike Abi and James who found their school placements to be miserable and draining experiences, Ellen talks excitedly about how much she learned. "I had the most inspiring mentor teacher," she says.

> She was up to date, constantly going to CPD, doing Singapore maths, doing research alongside her practice, building amazing relationships with the kids. She really helped me because she was just the right balance between nurturing me and helping me to feel confident, but also challenging me and critiquing me and helping me to move on.

Ellen talks passionately about how the often poor standards of teaching she observed in other classrooms during her placements only served to redouble her commitment to a career in the classroom. Her passion for teaching is unmistakable.

When a new cohort of thirty thousand trainee teachers near the end of their course, there is a mad scramble to find jobs for the new school year.[82] Like most trainees, Ellen was anxious to find a position. "I started quite early applying for jobs, because I was really nervous I wouldn't get one." She sat in the university library and wrote applications for seven different teaching positions in a single day, and was pleasantly surprised to hear back from one school within 24 hours. It was in an affluent area of North London, a short commute from her house, and was rated 'Outstanding' by Ofsted. It looked like a peach. Feeling flattered, and more than a little relieved, Ellen was quick to accept their invitation to an interview. Two days later she went to the school, expecting to be observed teaching and grilled by the leadership team. But it turned out to be far less taxing than she expected, and she was delighted to be offered a job the same day. "It all happened really, really quickly," she says, with a knowing intonation. She had readily accepted the position before any of the other schools had even responded to her application.

> The first day I got there – an inset day on the 1st of September – I met all these lovely staff members. But within ten minutes we had worked out that all of us – *every single one of us* – was new. We looked around and thought: what happened here? My heart just sank.

It turned out that Ellen's 'Outstanding' new school was actually so dysfunctional that every one of its classroom teachers had resigned the previous year, leaving only the two-man leadership team in place.

Gradually she understood why. Ellen explained how the school operated a surveillance culture, requiring each teacher to write a one-page plan for each maths and English lesson, which then had to be submitted, would be marked over the weekend before being returned, and then had to be revised in line with feedback before the lesson was taught. The workload was overwhelming. The leadership team would conduct unplanned lesson observations to ensure that teachers were sticking to the letter of the plans, forcing these inexperienced teachers to try and teach what they saw as an 'Ofsted Outstanding' lesson when they had nowhere near enough bandwidth to master all those techniques at once. As a result, Ellen would have to plan and revise an 'official' lesson plan for each lesson, the one with all the bells and whistles of complicated and differentiated activities to satisfy management. Alongside it, she would separately plan a more straightforward 'unofficial' lesson which she was capable of delivering competently. Book scrutiny was a regular occurrence, but little or no useful feedback was offered to teachers as a result, which left her in a state of chronic low confidence. During her first term, Ellen was forced to attend a mock Ofsted inspection despite being badly ill with shingles. Unsurprisingly, her performance during the lesson observation was not great. More surprisingly, given her condition and lack of experience, she was informed earnestly by the head that, if this had been a real inspection, her performance would have 'endangered the whole school'. Even Ellen is shocked by her story as she recounts it to me. "It was just awful," she says.

But Ellen's story is not simply about schools placing impossible demands on teachers, or failing to offer teachers the support they need. She is different from James and Abi in that, somehow, in spite of the way she was treated, she still wanted to be a teacher. "I did get better as a teacher, definitely," she says. "And I was happy when I was with the children. I loved it." But she knew she couldn't keep working in such a dysfunctional institution. Her friends and family were clear that the stress of working there was taking too heavy a toll on her health and private life. So, Ellen did what any of us would do in this situation and started looking for another school. But as she began combing through the job adverts in teacher magazines she began to wonder how she could distinguish the good schools from the dysfunctional ones. By this point, several of her colleagues had handed in their notice. She was therefore not surprised to see her own school advertising in the job pages. As she read the advert to replace her former colleagues – *Outstanding, North London, Church of England Primary School* – something struck her: "If I didn't know what this school was like, *I* would be interested in the job." In fact, the other teaching posts she had been circling as being of interest were indistinguishable on paper. Many good or outstanding schools hadn't been inspected for years, so Ofsted report descriptions were meaningless. She tried to find information about staff retention to form a judgment for herself, but there was nothing in the public realm. Indeed, by now she had come to realise something even more troubling: the very fact that these schools were recruiting was itself indicative of problems at the school. Could they not hang on to their staff? Eventually, reluctantly, Ellen concluded that she couldn't put herself through it. She knew there were good teaching jobs out there. She had a couple of friends who worked at excellent primary schools nearby. But, perhaps unsurprisingly, neither of them were hiring. "I couldn't take the risk of ending up in another school like my one."

So Ellen is no longer a teacher. For the last eight months she has been working at a social integration charity that breaks down barriers between pupils of different ethnic groups. She enjoys it, but doesn't go into much detail. "I'm still finding it hard to not to be a teacher" she says, almost sounding apologetic. "I do miss it. I just love working with school children. Sometimes when I see kids in their uniform going to school in the morning I could cry." She laughs nervously as she sees the sympathetic look spreading across my face. "I look at TES job vacancies most days, but it's just made me super sceptical." It is ironic bordering on tragic that, during a period of acute teacher shortages, a fully qualified teacher who would love to be back in the classroom feels unable to apply for a teaching job.

*   *   *

When George Akerlof was at elementary school, his older brother read a book on handwriting analysis and, after studying a passage of George's writing, promptly informed him that he had the handwriting of a murderer. In his autobiography, written some fifty years later, Akerlof points out that this prediction has "so far proven incorrect."[83] As well as illustrating the enduring nature of sibling rivalry, this comment is indicative of the thinking that would later win Akerlof a Nobel prize in economics.

Akerlof's research, beginning with his doctoral thesis at Yale, was marked by a concern to understand the rich variety of ways in which markets operate. He wanted to push beyond the simplifying assumptions of the economics he had been taught, in particular the idea that all buyers and sellers in a market have access to all the relevant information about the quality of the goods or services they are trading. He recognised that many real world transactions, like the market for teaching jobs in which Ellen was situated, are characterised by a severe lack of information. How well do markets work when some people have information and others do not? It is this careful attention to the information that buyers and sellers possess that is visible in his rejoinder to his older brother. Akerlof knew he hadn't murdered anyone yet, but had no information about what he would or wouldn't do in the future.

Shortly after finishing his PhD, Akerlof was appointed to an Assistant Professorship at Berkeley and began working on the thorny issue of markets and information via the somewhat unglamorous topic of the second-hand car market. He wanted to know what would happen when consumers couldn't distinguish a 'lemon' (American slang for a defective used car) from a 'peach' (a well-maintained, reliable used car). To the untrained consumer eye, all the cars on the forecourt of a dealership look identical: clean, polished, perfectly good during a short test drive. But some of them – the peaches – would run for years, with minimal need for further maintenance; others – the lemons – would begin to experience problems soon after they were driven off the forecourt. Akerlof's insight was that, as long as consumers couldn't distinguish the two, they would be willing to pay less than the full price for a peach. Why would they when they may well end up with a lemon? Indeed, the more lemons they thought there were among the cars on the forecourt, the less they would be willing to pay for any given car. In response, Akerlof realised, the garage owners would no longer be willing to sell peaches, since the highest price that consumers were willing to pay for any given car was now lower than the cost to the dealer of acquiring a peach. The end result is that car dealers, who can use their experienced eye to distinguish a peach from a lemon, choose to stop selling peaches all together and instead trade exclusively in lemons, for which consumers are willing to pay the (admittedly lower) asking price. This vicious downward spiral in quality, which ensures that only the worst cars go on sale, is known as adverse selection. Akerlof's insights were immortalised in his famous 1970 article, *The market for lemons.*[84]

Ellen learned about adverse selection the hard way. When she was applying for her first teaching job she thought that she could spot a peach just from the job advert, but it turned out that an Ofsted inspection from a few years ago was no more informative than the well-buffed paintwork on the second-hand cars. In reality, she had no idea what was going on under the bonnet of the schools listed on the job pages. She had nowhere near enough information to avoid a lemon. Looking back at the recruitment process, she can pick out some warning signs: the school was advertising for new teachers before the end of the school year, the near-immediate response to her application, the light-touch interview process, the hasty offer of a job. "It turns out the haste was just because they were desperate for anybody," she laments. Of course, even the best-managed schools have a degree of turnover due to retirement and the speedy administration of the recruitment process could equally be a sign of an efficiently managed school. During a time of severe teacher shortages, all schools need to move fast when it comes to recruitment. These subtle signals are easy to pick out in hindsight, but less so in the heat of the moment. That's why Ellen refuses to apply for another teaching job. The last lemon left such a sour taste that she can't bear to go back. Indeed, the experience has made her so suspicious that she now interprets the very fact that a school is advertising for a job as indicative of it being badly managed. It's the lemons, losing masses of teachers each year, which are most likely to be advertising.

* * *

Teachers aren't the only ones trying to avoid picking a lemon in the job market. Headteachers are facing the equal and opposite problem: trying to recruit the most effective teachers. In Akerlof's car market the dealers have no trouble distinguishing the peaches from the lemons. They can use their knowledge of engine mechanics to look under the bonnet to differentiate the two. However, two different strands of research suggest that headteachers do not enjoy the same *full information* when interviewing teachers.

Susan and Clarrie are two highly experienced headteachers, who between them have run several schools and hired hundreds of teachers. They talk in a calm, fair but firm tone that is uncannily similar to the way my headteacher used to speak to us. I ask them how they go about trying to avoid ineffective teachers when hiring. What do they look for? The first thing they say is that it is difficult, if not impossible, to tell the difference by just looking at a CV. "It's the human characteristics that matter," says Susan. There is plenty of research that agrees with our heads hard-won wisdom. Economists spent years trying to identify the characteristics of the teachers whose pupils make most progress. None of the obvious characteristics – masters degrees, quality of university attended, training route – seem to make much of a difference.[85] Even subject knowledge – something it can be hard for headteachers to measure – is only found to be related to teacher effectiveness when certain instructional methods are used.[86]

Of course, paper credentials are not the only thing that headteachers have to inform their hiring choices. Interviews are perceived to be an important part of the process, but research tells us it is hard to use them to assess knowledge or pedagogical skills.[87] As a result, teaching interviews focus heavily on the personalities and behaviours that *can* be measured: enthusiasm, motivation, honesty, caring nature and emotional stability.[88]

Most headteachers also believe that classroom observations at interview are critical to judging teacher quality, and Clarrie asserts it gives her "a huge advantage in making the right choice." However, given that the validity of a single, short lesson observation has been undermined by recent research studies, we must be sceptical about how useful they really are in the artificial environment of the interview.[89]

What Clarrie can recall was "the days when most of us had a plethora of applications, so we could be quite selective and bring in a number of ways to assess their potential during the process." This might involve accepting more placement students in to observe them in the classroom, or bringing teachers in to teach trial lessons, then taking time to reflect with them on what they could have improved about the lessons to assess their ability for self-criticism. Employing new teachers on one-year contracts was another option. But the shortage of teachers means these methods of assessing a teacher's aptitude are no longer feasible. "Increasingly what we do is appoint very rapidly. We are dragging them off the street," she laughs.

> It used to be that you tried to recruit them on their second training placement when it was clear what sort of teacher they were likely to be. Now it has become on their first placement because their second school will certainly take them if you haven't. Often they have been appointed by the end of November.

Susan nods in agreement. "The key skill has become spotting talent in inexperienced, unrefined teachers – spotting potential. I have definitely become better at this over time. But I still make mistakes."

The difficulty of spotting peaches means that often very effective teachers will be rejected at job interviews and so may find themselves without an appointment. This curiosity became apparent in 1996 when the state of California decided to hire thousands of teachers to reduce class sizes to below twenty. It meant that they tripled the number of teacher recruitments they made that year, with the consequence that many who would not have found employment in a normal year had to be employed under the new policy. Researchers showed that, despite this (and controlling for the reduction in class sizes brought about by the policy), Californian schools were no less effective after the policy was introduced. This strongly suggests that heads were not managing to select the best teachers before the expansion in the workforce.[90]

Both Clarrie and Susan are quick to emphasise the costs of getting a hiring decision wrong. Indeed, the danger of getting it wrong is perhaps even higher for heads because, unlike a teacher who can choose to leave a bad school, a head cannot easily reverse their decision to give somebody a permanent contract. "I am really committed to professional development and learning for all teachers. I really do believe you can grow good teachers," explains Susan.

> But at some point you have to think about your kids and say "no more". When your science results are bad for the third year running

and you still have teachers who won't teach the kids adequately and won't mark the books, they have got to go.

It is clear that neither of them would take the decision to sack a teacher lightly. "It is time consuming, difficult, draining, and distressing. That's the most shocking experience of headship." Clarrie, who has successfully turned around two failing schools during her career, recalled her astonishment when she first tried to remove a teacher on the grounds of capability and was told by both the union and the local authority that the best way to do so would be through a 'compromise agreement'. This involved paying them a lump sum and signing a mutually agreed, inaccurate, overly positive reference that would allow them to find employment in another school.

That came as a real shock to me. I thought that was unethical, I didn't want to do it, I didn't want to recycle those poor teachers into the system. But over a period of time I learned that that was the only way of getting them out of my school and bringing good people in.

Susan nods as she says: "None of us can talk about this. You are all gagged afterwards."

Employment protection is a valuable feature of living and working in the UK, and there is a difficult balance to be struck when considering procedures for the dismissal of very weak teachers. Indeed, in recent years the time it takes to put a teacher through capability processes has shortened considerably.[91] But even with these strengthened powers for heads now in place, both Clarrie and Susan say they still know of heads who will give terrible teachers a glowing reference in order to get rid of them. Of course, an experienced headteacher can spot the subtle signs of an agreed reference – the bland language, which is light on specific details of the teacher's qualities. But many still miss these signals. The ultimate irony is that this apparently common practice only serves to make the headteacher's job harder, since even positive references no longer reliably convey information about the quality of an applicant.

The difficulty of spotting peaches may be producing another phenomenon that we see on the car forecourt – depressed prices. Just as car buyers are unwilling to pay a good price for a quality car, just in case it turns out to be a lemon, our headteachers are unwilling to offer a high wage to hire a talented teacher. Similarly, outstanding teachers find it hard to bargain for pay rises in existing jobs, for their current employer knows they can command no more than a 'lemon' wage if they look elsewhere. Some economists argue this is why we observe many of the most effective teachers leaving teaching in large numbers (at least in the US) – the only way they can secure the pay rise they feel they deserve is to quit teaching by moving to another sector or quit teaching by getting promoted to management.[92]

The inability to observe teacher quality in the labour market explains why universal pay scales persist, even though the government has encouraged differential pay.[93] All this traps us in a low-wage and low-quality equilibrium. We can only change this situation by making it more transparent who the weak teachers in the marketplace are. Many professions do a much better job at restricting entry at the start of careers, through tough recruitment and accreditation hurdles. Teaching has long been in a situation where all trainees are awarded qualified teacher status because the government incentivised teacher-training institutions to recruit trainees to fill quotas and then judged the quality of courses on proportions awarded qualified teacher status. There is little point in trying to fix this while we have a chronic teacher shortage: having 'a-body' at the front of the classroom is better than 'no-body' teaching the children.[94] So, knowing we have lemons in our market, it is imperative that we do more to support efficient hiring practices.

I tell Susan and Clarrie about what happened at Ellen's school, with all the classroom teachers leaving two years in a row. They exchange knowing glances with each other and Susan tells me:

> I could name two schools right now that are going through that. Staff have voted with their feet after a major change; the schools are in a very difficult position. But I know that they have recruited madly and I do not know if the school has the capacity to train those teachers appropriately, expertly, in the way that it needs to.

It's worth reflecting on what this amounts to. In the course of two interviews, we have been told about three schools that are systematically recruiting naïve, often inexperienced new teachers, knowing full well that they do not have the capacity to support them and help them develop into capable teachers. The result, as we saw in Chapter 3, is that these teachers will likely never develop the skills necessary to become teachers, never achieve the sense of success that we all crave at work, may become burned out and will likely end up leaving the profession as a result. Then in the following year these schools will recruit another batch of naïve, inexperienced teachers and do the same thing. They are essentially sausage machines, efficiently grinding the fresh meat from teacher training programmes into a gristly paste. I explain to Clarrie and Susan the effect that this had on Ellen who, despite wanting to get back into the classroom, is now too suspicious to apply for a teaching job. The tragedy of this is not lost on the two headteachers, who both spend a lot of their time searching high and low for new teachers. It is clear they empathise with her predicament. Clarrie explains that she will rarely employ a supply teacher, even if they appear to be a great teacher. "They have to be extremely good to overcome scepticism of why they are doing supply teaching to begin with. I know through compromise agreements that lots of them go there." Like Ellen, she has learned that there are just too many lemons on that forecourt.

*   *   *

In 2003 Brian Jacob, from the University of Michigan, and Lars Lefgren, from Brigham Young University in Utah, conducted a ground breaking new study. They wanted to find out how well headteachers understood the effectiveness of the teachers in their own schools.[95] So they sent a letter to every headteacher in a nearby school district and asked them to confidentially rate all of the teachers in their school on their ability to raise pupil attainment, using a scale stretching from 0 (inadequate) to 10 (exceptional). The heads were free to use any information available to them in the school: classroom observations, student test scores or feedback from parents. The average rating given by a head was just over 8, but there was also considerable variation, with 10 per cent of teachers being rated less than 6.5 and more than 10 per cent being given the top score. Jacob and Lefgren then used sophisticated techniques, not available to headteachers, to objectively measure pupil progress made in classes. The researchers divided the teachers into two categories based on their objective rating – the most effective 50 per cent and the least effective 50 per cent – and looked at how likely a headteacher was to accurately rate one of their most effective teachers as being in the top 50 per cent. They found that the headteachers were about three times more accurate than we would expect from uninformed guesswork. They were just as effective at picking out the very least effective teachers. So while the California heads were unable to reliably distinguish quality when recruiting new teachers, heads seem quite capable of identifying teacher quality in their own school, at least at the extreme ends of the distribution.

Heads reading this book will likely not be surprised by this. As Susan put it to us, "In a year, you can pretty much tell [how good they are]." But the research helps bring into sharp focus an important distinction which is not well understood in the world of education. Economists distinguish internal labour markets, which involve hiring or promoting somebody from within the organisation, from external labour markets, which involve hiring somebody employed elsewhere. The main difference, Akerlof would point out, is the amount of information available to the decision maker. Hiring teachers straight from training programmes, from other schools or from supply agencies increases the chance that you will pick a peach. When the teacher has worked in the school for a while, heads have a chance to kick the tyres and have a good look under the bonnet. They become more like the second hand car dealers, able to reliably distinguish the peaches. And it works both ways. It is only by working in a school that teachers can check whether the school is a dysfunctional lemon or a well-managed, caring institution, capable of supporting their development and professional growth. The irony, as we have already seen, is that the teacher shortage is pushing schools into greater reliance on the external labour market, recruiting teachers before they have had a chance to observe their potential through training placements and temporary contracts and relying instead on paper credentials or hunches. This is of course damaging for schools, who end up spending scarce time, money and energy hiring and firing. But more importantly it is damaging for pupils, some of whom end up with poor teachers who have snuck into their schools using their positive but inaccurate 'agreed' references. Clarrie's comment about recycling poor teachers through the system by giving them an inflated reference is known by economists, following Akerlof's work, as the 'dance of the lemons'. Round and round they go.

All this only reinforces the need to tackle the teacher shortage. A sufficient supply of teachers would allow schools to spend more time carefully assessing the quality of applicants, rather than 'dragging them off the street'. Chapter 3 suggested some promising methods for tackling the supply shortage by improving working conditions and retention for early-career teachers. But at present, dysfunctional schools like the one that employed Ellen are able to continue treating their new early-career teachers abysmally year after year precisely because they are indistinguishable from good schools in the external labour market. They operate safe in the knowledge that a fresh batch of teachers will unwittingly throw themselves into the sausage machine every September. Wider reforms to the way teachers are trained and recruited are therefore needed to stop the slaughter.

Recent reforms have indeed expanded schools' ability to recruit through internal labour markets. The proportion of initial teacher training places allocated to school-based routes, in which trainees spend more time working in schools, has increased from 20 per cent in 2011 to 56 per cent in 2017.[96] Just over a third of NQTs now find their first job in a school in which they have already worked, i.e. through the internal labour market.[97] The explosive growth in multi-academy trusts has also helped expand the boundaries of the internal labour market. Headteachers from within the same academy chain are better able to gather honest appraisals of teachers from other schools in the trust by simply picking up the phone to their counterpart. It should therefore be easy to stop poor teachers being recycled within the same multi-academy trust. Entire teacher careers can be fashioned through promotions within the same trust and research has shown that this is increasingly the way that trusts are operating.[98]

Of course, this does not solve the issue of schools writing agreed references for teachers and then offloading them onto unwitting schools outside of the trust. The expansion of internal labour markets up until now has therefore helped to increase the information available to heads, but only within limits.

For teachers like Ellen, who are not currently teaching, this internal labour market created by trusts is of little help because it provides no signal as to which *schools* are lemons. However, researchers like us, who work with England's School Workforce Census, can spot schools that might be running, knowingly or otherwise, a 'recruit–burnout–replace' staffing model. These schools have unusually high teacher turnover over a number of years, but we prefer to look closely at the turnover of their early career staff in particular. The advantage of monitoring the burnout of newly qualified teachers (NQTs) is that they less frequently leave schools because of promotions, retirements or family circumstances. This means high NQT burnout should almost always be a cause for concern. [99]

When we count the proportion of NQTs who have chosen to leave a school at the end of the year, we can see that some schools have lost every single one of the NQTs they employed over a five-year period and others have kept every single one. This raises the question of how much variation in NQT loss it is reasonable to see in the data, given that small schools may only employ them very infrequently. Fortunately, this question has already been answered by Professor David Spiegelhalter, who introduced funnel plots to make meaningful comparisons between hospitals. [100]

The figure below plots the proportion of NQTs who leave a school over a five-year period against the number of NQTs the school employed, for each secondary school in the North West of England. The funnel plot lines on the chart allow us to see what sort of school variation in turnover rates is to be expected given chance process and which schools fall outside the boundaries of this expected variation. On the chart, there are 22 secondary schools out of 458 in the North West that have seen NQTs leave at unexpectedly high rates over the past five years. We calculate that there are 122 such schools in the country. It is in these schools that we are worried that there might

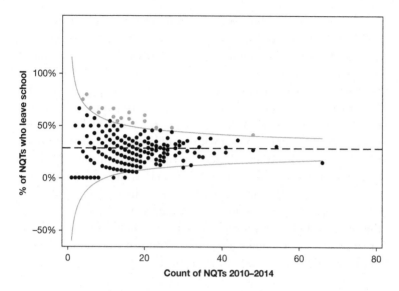

FIGURE 4.1 Proportion of NQTs who leave a school over a five-year period (secondary schools in the North West region)

Adapted from Allen, R. & Sims, S. (2018)

be some systematic policies or behaviours that are leading to employee disquiet and thus high turnover.

Having analysed this teacher turnover data carefully, there is then the question of what should be done with it. Our goals here are two-fold. We want to ensure schools are incentivised to treat staff well and only take on NQTs if they feel they can support them. But we also want to use the data to support those schools who are clearly struggling. A soft policy could simply involve passing this data back to school governors or onto Regional Schools Commissioners who could broker school support, perhaps from nearby schools with a good track record.

A more radical option would be to make information on early career retention freely available to newly qualified teachers so that they can take it into account when making decisions about where to take jobs. This is similar to the market for new solicitors, where retention rates for different law firms are published by trade magazines and serve as an influential signal of how attractive different firms are to work for.[101] Solicitors firms take retention very seriously as a result. An equivalent measure for schools would have to be constructed carefully to adjust for the fact that high turnover is not always bad – it often rises during successful school 'turnaround' efforts, for example.[102] We also need to ensure it does not discourage schools from taking on 'risky' novice teachers that we value despite greater risk of leaving. Our research, for example, has shown that older career changing novice teachers and those from ethnic minorities are both more likely to leave the profession early on. [103] Nevertheless, this additional information would help teachers avoid schools like Ellen's and allow them to apply for jobs, confident in the knowledge that they can avoid the lemons. Indeed, over time this policy should force down the proportion of bad schools altogether. You can't operate a sausage machine if there's no fresh meat to put in.

Things that schools can do without waiting for policymakers

- Exploit your own internal labour market because this is where you know which teachers you value the most. One of the most important jobs a headteacher has is to make sure a career plan is in place for the teachers they most want to retain.

- Expand your own internal labour market. Of course, sharing the expertise of staff is not a good enough reason, on its own, to form a multi-academy trust. Instead, an *ad-hoc* group of local schools can work together to create career paths for valued teachers and commit to sharing honest intelligence about the quality of teachers.

- Where job vacancies do arise, consider all options before placing a job advert into a marketplace where you cannot easily observe quality. Try to anticipate future staffing needs and use teacher training routes to 'try out' potential recruits. Encourage all your senior staff to build a pool of teachers they 'know', through courses or otherwise. Use this pool of teachers to help you find reliable new hires when vacancies arise.

- Fill the information deficit as much as possible when making external hires. Do not trust written references. Instead, call up former employers and ask them questions about prospective hires – about teacher absence, behaviour management, collegiality, subject knowledge and teaching evaluations. Specificity of questions encourages honesty. For example, 'did your teacher observations and pupil test data suggest this teacher was (i) one of the strongest in your school; (ii) in the top half of performance; (iii) in the lower half of performance; (iv) one of the weakest teachers in your school?'. In return, be a good citizen and encourage other headteachers to call you up for a verbal reference on those you have previously employed.

- Teachers, if you decide to apply to teach at a new school, make sure it isn't a lemon. Given the teacher shortage, you should be in a position to be more picky. Before your interview, ask existing colleagues or tutors what they know about the school. If you can find the time for a school visit before the interview, this often helps you learn what the school is typically like. During your interview day, do ask how many teachers left the school last year. Ask existing staff you meet during the day how long they have been at the school and ask about their typical working hours.

- Ross McGill has written about the future of lesson observations at interview, proposing an alternative approach whereby teachers build up their own portfolio of evidence. This could include a video of a lesson observation, portfolios of CPD attended, student, parent and colleagues' comments, and so on.[104] Whether you are a teacher or school leader, consider whether this approach could support better recruitment or promotions in the future.

CHAPTER FIVE

Teacher motivation
You couldn't pay me to do that

In Chapter 3, we saw how teachers are leaving the profession because they are working in schools that impede their climb up the dizzyingly steep early stages of their learning curve. This chapter looks at what happens to the group of teachers who manage to stick it out and achieve that all-important 'sense of success.'[105] Around six in ten trainees make it to this stage. They have done well to make the climb, but having white-knuckled it through the first few years of their career they are now faced with the realisation that they are only at base camp. There is a long – potentially decades-long – route ahead of them. To keep climbing will take all their energy, and plateauing at this stage will be just as disappointing. It is therefore critical that we keep teachers motivated.

Unfortunately, the evidence suggests we are not. Surveys generally find that around a third of teachers claim to be disengaged from their work or have low morale, with another third being merely ambivalent about their jobs. Fully two thirds of teachers who have been in profession for five years or more say their morale has declined in the last two years.[106] The number that say they are considering leaving in the next year has also jumped from 17 per cent to around 25 per cent. Of course, not all those considering leaving will end up leaving, but it is hardly a ringing endorsement of teachers' satisfaction at work. The number who actually manage to leave has increased from 6 per cent per annum in 2011 to just over 8 per cent in 2016 (these figures exclude retirees).[107] This is a huge problem for policymakers looking to close the teacher gap.

One common response is performance-related pay. The logic is obvious: provide teachers with powerful incentives to improve their practice and help keep the best ones in the process. This idea is certainly not new. Piece-rate pay for teachers has been around in England, on and off, for as long as mass schooling itself. In 1858, The Duke of Newcastle was appointed "To inquire into the state of public education in England and to consider and report what measures, if any, are required for the extension of sound and cheap elementary instruction to all classes of the people."[108] He recommended a system of performance-related pay, and the government began to fund schools based on the results achieved by their pupils in reading, writing and arithmetic across six 'standards', which roughly became the six year groups of elementary schools.[109] This newly devised performance-related pay for teachers was described by Robert Lowe, Palmerstone's Vice President of the Privy Council, in Parliament as a system where the taxpayer could not lose:

> I cannot promise the House that this system will be an economical one and I cannot promise that it will be an efficient one, but I can promise that it shall be one or the other. If it is not cheap it shall be efficient; if it is not efficient it shall be cheap.[110]

The scheme did indeed seem sensible in an era where many children either did not go to school or attended only irregularly. This new payment would ensure schools raised pupil attendance and lowered levels of illiteracy, which were still shockingly high at the time.[111]

Wind forward 150 years, to December 2012, and the government was again announcing that all schools should put in place a perform-ance-related pay (PRP) scheme to "make teaching a more attractive career and a more rewarding job."[112] Nationally agreed pay scales for teachers in England and Wales would be scrapped and schools were given discretion as to how they chose to implement these schemes so that they could be "tailored to their particular needs." Schools were thus left with the risky task of devising a system of incentives that would energise their staff to improve their teaching practice and keep them in the classroom. Faced with the requirement to introduce a PRP scheme, whether they liked it or not, many schools deliberately steered as close as possible to the *status quo* with schemes that presume all teachers will move up the pay scale in an orderly fashion, unless something is amiss.[113] However, many schools saw this as an opportunity to devise detailed performance management and pay schemes that try to measure and incentivise exactly the sorts of behaviour they wanted from their teachers.

Luke is an English teacher in one such school. He studied creative writing at university and, after a few years bouncing between different jobs after graduation, decided to train as an English teacher with Teach First. He is short, dark haired and speaks quickly. "I wanted to pass on my love of the subject," he explains when I ask why. His friends also encouraged him to apply because they thought he would be good at the job. Luke has now been working at his school, which gets some of the best GCSE results in the region, for two and half years. But even during this short time he has seen big changes: "When I started, performance management was more or less based on how good you were in the classroom, based on classroom observations, but now it's all different." Most notably, starting this academic year, for Luke to be awarded a pay rise, he must submit written evidence of "increased, sustained and consistent" achievement on six criteria: high quality teaching and learning; positive impact on pupil progress; impact on wider outcomes for pupils; specific elements of teaching practice; contribution to the work of the school; and impact on the effectiveness of colleagues and staff. In addition to providing written evidence on these six criteria, his pay is conditional on achieving target GCSE grades for each year 11 pupil he teaches, as well as running extra-curricular activities and taking part in a "learning community." Luke is one of thousands of teachers whose pay rises are now contingent on their performance.

We know quite a lot about the effects of these pay schemes because public school districts in the US and elsewhere have been experimenting with them for the past 30 years. They have been able to do so because they have a longer history of trying to measure annual pupil learning gains.[114] Some PRP schemes have even been introduced as randomised controlled trials (RCT) allowing us to isolate the effect of paying teachers in this way. Perhaps surprisingly, the evidence on how PRP schemes affect outcomes – usually the students' performance in standardised tests – is rather mixed. There are positive findings, but equally many neutral or negative findings that cannot easily be explained away by scheme design or the wider accountability environment.[115] These results are mirrored by mixed findings for the effectiveness of PRP across the public sector, including in health and the civil service.[116]

There are circumstances where PRP has improved teacher performance. Washington DC introduced new payments for very high performing teachers alongside the threat of dismissal for poorly performing teachers. Research shows that pupil outcomes improved as a result; this is likely because the weakest teachers chose to leave schools even before they were dismissed.[117] Minnesota introduced a scheme rather like the English system, with schools given flexibility over design of the pay system. It improved test scores in reading, but not in maths.[118] Professor Victor Lavy, from Warwick University, has also studied a PRP scheme in Israel which he found to have a positive effect, including measureable changes in classroom instructional techniques.[119] And in England, economists from the University of Bristol found that the introduction of the "threshold assessment" for the Upper Pay Scale in the late nineties was associated with improved pupil attainment in the classrooms of the teachers who were eligible to apply.[120]

But for every PRP scheme that appears to successfully raise pupil achievement we can find another that does not. For example, an RCT in Nashville, Tennessee, which provided teachers with large bonuses of up to $15k for student improvements in mathematics had no effects on student performance, teacher effort, or classroom practice.[121] An RCT in New York City, which gave teachers rewards of up to $3k for meeting performance targets found no positive, and even some negative, effects on student outcomes.[122] An RCT in Chicago which gave rewards of up to $6.4k based on a mix of a student performance improvement measures (value-added scores), class observations, and teachers' involvement in the school found no significant impacts.[123] Another RCT in the Chicago Heights also showed no positive impact of giving teachers up to $8k for good student test performance. However, another part of the same experiment did show teachers responded to potential loss in pay: they gave teachers a bonus at the start of the year alongside a contract requiring them to give it back if they their students did not perform sufficiently well.[124]

This research tells us that sometimes pupil attainment improves if PRP is introduced; sometimes it doesn't. Equally importantly, this research tells us that PRP schemes frequently lead to underhand behaviour. Some US schemes led schools to game the system, finding ways to boost the attainment of pupils without actually improving the quality of education provided. This included disproportionately focusing resources on the performance of 'borderline' pupils who are close to meeting the targets, at the expense of other pupils, or moving the more effective teachers into the year groups that are subject to accountability.[125] More seriously, in these high-stakes situations, schools have conspired to alter students' test scores.[126] Luke told us how his feeder primary school, under pressure from Ofsted to improve grades, had inflated their KS2 exam results:

> These targets for the kids in my class are based on KS2 results, which are mostly false. They are nowhere near that level. I've got kids in my class targeted Grade 8 (A*), but they can't form sentences properly, can't write in paragraphs. I asked them what happened during their SATS and they said their teachers were pointing to the right answers on their exam paper. Even if we put 100% of our time into just these Year 11 kids, trying to achieve these targets, we wouldn't.

Survey data from England suggests that maladministration of age 11 SATs tests could be widespread. One in three primary teachers who have been involved in test administration say they have, or have been asked to, carry out practices that might distort pupil performance. These include providing an unwarranted reader or scribe under the pretence of 'normal practice', allowing the class extra time, giving instructions such as spellings in a 'helpful' way or pointing out an incorrect answer to a child. Luke's experience as a secondary school teacher in hearing stories of maladministration is quite common: the same survey reports that 29 per cent of secondary teachers have heard such stories.[127]

It was just this sort of gaming that slowly caused the collapse of the 1870 system of 'payment by results'. The curriculum became restricted to the 'three Rs' (plus needlework), ignoring the needs of the brightest children. They taught to the test, drilled, physically beat the slower kids or even cheated to ensure they could satisfy the inspector and receive the money.[128] After years of relaxing the scheme to remove its most deleterious effects, it was finally abandoned by the Board of Education around the turn of the century. This same type of gaming now threatens Luke's pay.

Economists are great at coming up with explanations for why their PRP scheme hasn't worked, but the next one will. They will say that the test score targets were too ambitious. They will say they were weakly powered because the scheme was group-based, leading some teachers to slack off and rely on the efforts of others. They will say that the incentives were linked to an outcome over which the teacher didn't perceive they had full control. They will argue that teachers were not given the support and resources to respond to the incentives. They will suggest that if we let the scheme run for longer it would attract higher-quality teachers to the school, and so on. These are exactly the responses you should make if you believe in 'homo economicus', the rational and self-interested person optimally pursuing his well-defined goals.[129] A rational person will always respond to incentives, so a lack of response suggests that the problem lies with the incentives. However, research about the fundamentals of human nature suggests that the problem with offering PRP to teachers may run far deeper than the administrative or operational details of the way a particular scheme has been implemented.

To make sense of why PRP seems to fail as often as it succeeds, and to understand how we can better motivate teachers, we need to look instead to psychology. There are a number of competing theories which can help explain what motivates teachers including expectancy-value theory, achievement-goal theory and self-determination theory.[130] All three help shed light on different aspects of teacher motivation. The first, for example, has been used to show that teachers' initial motivations to teach are mainly the intrinsic value they place on teaching and perceived abilities together with altruistic attitudes. Measuring these motivations at the outset of teachers' careers has been shown to predict several measures of teacher retention.[131] The second, achievement goal theory, distinguishes between teachers who are motivated by mastering their craft, and are therefore willing to ask for help and to make mistakes in order to learn, and those with the desire to outperform others, who tend to avoid situations in which they fear they will be shown up. This will resonate with many newly qualified teachers who have felt the need to avoid being known to their peers as the one with the out-of-control classes! This theory has been used in empirical research to show, for example, that teachers who are motivated by mastery rather than performance goals are more engaged with their work and less likely to burn out.[132]

But it is the third of these theories that is most useful in helping us to understand motivation in the more experienced teacher. Self-determination theory (SDT) views humans as being naturally curious, born with a motivation to explore our environment in order to learn and develop new skills. But if this is true, and humans are all naturally highly motivated, how could we possibly have a problem with teacher motivation in the first place? The answer provided by SDT is that our environment can sometimes supress this natural desire to learn and grow. In particular, it states that all humans, including teachers, have three basic psychological needs. We need to feel *competence* in the sense of demonstrating and improving our abilities, *relatedness* in the sense of being valued, respected, and desired by others and *autonomous* in the sense that we are the authors of our own actions. According to the theory, when these three things – sometimes referred to as nutrients – are present, humans express their natural, intrinsic motivation to develop and grow. Where they are absent, humans will become demotivated and disengage from their work. For some readers, this theorising might sound a little far-fetched. But the evidence for SDT has been steadily building for decades and there is good empirical evidence that the satisfaction of these three basic psychological needs do indeed increase intrinsic motivation,[133] including among teachers.[134]

From this perspective, the teacher motivation problem starts to look very different indeed. The problem is not, as the apologetic economists would have us believe, the absence of the correct incentives. Rather, it is the absence of the three basic psychological needs that undermine the intrinsic drive to become a better teacher. For some, like Ellen in Chapter 4, it is the lack of autonomy created by micro-managing school leaders forcing her to write out detailed plans for every lesson, which she would then have to revise to fit with the leadership view of what constituted a good lesson. For others, like James in Chapter 3, it was the absence of a sense of competence that resulted from being forced to teach outside his subject specialism. And for his friend Abi, it was the lack of connectedness she felt, isolated in her temporary classroom, that sapped her energy. Indeed, all three of these teachers spontaneously mentioned each of the three basic psychological needs being lacking to some extent at their schools. And all three of them responded in the way that SDT predicts they would: they left their jobs to try and satisfy these needs outside of teaching.[135]

That Abi, James and Ellen weren't given the support they needed to thrive in the classroom highlights the lack of leadership skill present in their schools. But what is happening at Luke's school goes a step further, since the PRP scheme imposed by the leadership to motivate staff is doing precisely the opposite. The inflated progress targets on which he is judged, based on unreliable Key Stage 2 grades, make him feel destined to fail: "Even with 100% focus on year 11 I don't think we would be able to get them where we need to get them . . . So we're just getting a lot of spreadsheets handed over to us, saying these kids are in the red." As you can imagine, this has had quite an effect on his sense of competence. "When you're not reaching your target, even though some great learning has happened in your lessons, it makes that learning feel meaningless," he tells me. Empirical evidence suggests that Luke is, in all likelihood, a better teacher than he was in his first year at the school, but the introduction of the PRP scheme has left him feeling less competent than before. The additional workload involved in collecting and submitting evidence against the many different criteria on which he is judged has also reduced his time for working with other teachers.

However, by far the most damaging effect on the PRP scheme is on his autonomy as a teacher. Edward Deci and Richard Ryan, the two main progenitors of SDT, contrast autonomous action with controlled action, which is "performed to satisfy an external demand" and "reflects the degree to which one feels coerced or seduced by external contingencies."[136] It is clear that Luke sees the whole PRP system as something imposed on him from above by management. "The numbers and targets have become something a bit weird and quite alien. It says your progress target is 0.57," he says. "But if I was to turn round to a kid and say 'what does that mean?', they wouldn't have a clue. *I* barely have a clue. It's just a weird number that we have to aim for." Luke feels an overwhelming pressure to focus on a target, which does not necessarily distort how he chooses to teach; what it does do is distort how he feels about what he is doing. He asks me:

> Are we supposed to be instilling a love of learning, or is our job just to get data to feed spreadsheets? It's a shame because I really, genuinely do love being in the classroom, teaching. Actually seeing them enjoying themselves in the lesson – even if we are doing Shakespeare – seeing them show enjoyment for literature, is an amazing thing to do.

Luke now feels completely demotivated by the way in which he is being managed and rewarded and is looking to leave teaching by the end of the academic year. This is not surprising. There are over one hundred experiments assessing the effect of extrinsic incentives on intrinsic motivation and two separate meta-analysis of these studies have concluded that schemes like Luke's destroy intrinsic motivation.[137]

> It's just constantly being berated for not meeting targets, constantly being drawn into data meetings . . .. The teachers I talk to in the

school just seem to be depressed now, like they have had the energy sucked out of them.

* * *

As well as being a natural, sustainable resource, autonomous motivation turns out to be a powerful performance enhancer. Early studies compared whether controlled or autonomous motivation were more effective in helping people to achieve different goals and showed the latter to be more effective in achieving a range of personal goals from student exam attainment[138], to weight loss[139], smoking cessation[140], and physical exercise[141]. There are now over a hundred published studies looking at the links between the three basic psychological needs, autonomous motivation and performance. These have been summarised in two recent meta-analyses which both find a consistent and fairly strong positive relationship.[142] Research on teacher satisfaction in this field is still young, but a recent study has shown that school culture and teacher job satisfaction are together associated with higher student achievement in both maths and reading.[143]

So how can we nurture and make the most of teachers' autonomous motivation, beyond scrapping damaging PRP schemes? One obvious place to start is with school leadership. Several studies, including our own in England, have found links between management styles and teacher retention.[144] Professor John Marshall Reeve, who worked with Deci and Ryan at the University of Rochester as a postgraduate, has conducted experiments in real organisations to understand whether managers can be trained to do just this. In one of these experiments, he worked with a Fortune 500 manufacturing company and randomly assigned half of the participating managers to receive two, one-hour training sessions in which they were told about self-determination theory, discussed examples of autonomy-supportive management interactions and then came back together a week later to discuss how they had applied what they had learned in interactions with their employees. Along with his collaborator, Phillipa Hardre, Reeve then used a series of questionnaires to compare changes in managers' leadership styles and employees' motivation.

The results showed that, five weeks after completing the training, managers became more autonomy-supportive in their leadership style and their employees showed higher levels of intrinsic or autonomous motivation, relative to the control group. Since then, Reeve has also published a meta-analysis including eighteen other studies which shows that short interventions like this have consistently positive effects on employees' autonomous motivation. A little knowledge can therefore go a long way in improving leadership practices within schools and harnessing teachers desire to stay and improve.

There are many school leadership teams out there already adept in practising autonomy-supportive leadership. At Heathfield Community College, Caroline Barlow and her team have been relinquishing control through accountability and replacing it with a system of trust that gives teachers time to re-focus on their own professional development. Despite being one of the most poorly funded schools in the country, they have managed to introduce collaboration time into teachers' timetables where teachers choose activities to focus on their own personal development of teaching and learning, guided by a staff pedagogy team (who are not part of the leadership team). They share these discussions through an in-school blog and annual Teach Meet that promotes collaborative professional learning and reflects a common school culture.[145] This leadership of professional development rather than accountability has ignited a desire to get better at teaching in many of their staff, who increasingly choose to read education books from the staff library or attend conferences in their spare time.[146] The approach that Caroline has taken at Heathfield Community College is not just better for teachers; research shows it is better for the pupils too. Teachers and schools that engage in better quality collaboration have better achievement gains in maths and reading. Moreover, teachers improve at greater rates when they work in schools with better collaboration quality.[147]

Besides improving the quality of leadership within schools, teachers are increasingly working together *across* schools, feeding their basic psychological needs for relatedness. Alex Quigley, a teacher from York, explains how he found himself demotivated after a few years in the classroom.

My early career plateau would best be described as under-challenged burnout. I had mastered the difficult challenges of managing the behaviour of my students, in the main. I had developed my typical routines. But beyond that, few experiences excited me to develop my practice. A training day here or there would spark my interest, but I was neck deep in the job again the following day so the spark was snuffed out.[148]

But then something changed. "Twitter was the first and only time that I had contact with other teachers outside the school and local authority structures," he says.

People were talking about their teaching, about politics and about curriculum changes the day they were announced, not months later. It was quite a shock to find this community of teachers talking about the things I wanted to talk about, giving me answers or just having arguments. It led to me reading blogs and buying a few books. I quickly realised how little I knew and so I just hoovered up information. And then I started blogging because I wanted to be part of the conversation.

Tom Bennett, another prominent edu-tweeter who has gone on to advise the government on classroom behaviour, had a similar experience:

One of the first things I remember is discovering these teachers who were critical of progressive ideals on Twitter such as Andrew Old and Katherine Birbalsingh. I wasn't sure what I thought of their ideas but I remember thinking Andrew was a great writer and very rational. I suspect there was an 'Andrew Old' in every school: someone sceptical of the status quo who loves myth busting and research. But they were hermits within their school.

Twitter has transformed these scattered hermits into one big connected community, debating and discussing whatever issues they think are most interesting and receiving recognition for their expertise as they do. And this amazing virtual community of teachers has quickly moved back into real life interactions, with Tom Bennett setting up the researchED conferences that have now hosted events in countries across the globe. The new Chartered College of Teaching, meanwhile, aims to be a professional body for teachers in England. It gives teachers access to educational research and looks at ways of providing pathways of professional development. Both these organisations are important parts of a whole eco-system of grass-roots conferences, TeachMeets, blog series and twitter hashtag chats helping teachers reconnect with their love for the job in their own way.

Luke's school did understand that connectedness matters, so put their teachers to work in groups on professional development projects. However, Luke couldn't do it on his own terms: the school chose the project topic and the teachers that he must work with. Furthermore, they did all this through the means of controlled motivation, with project outcomes linked to performance appraisal and pay. If only they had asked him what he wanted to do to improve his teaching practice. For if they had, they might have seen his face light up, as it did when he explained to me that he would love to work with two other colleagues in the media department on structuring creative writing exercises. Like many other humans, Luke just wanted to have the time and space to choose how he works on improving his teaching, alongside others.

*   *   *

Trying to motivate teachers with performance-related pay is like trying to restart a car which has run out of petrol by topping up the battery. It is missing the point. We have seen in this chapter how teachers, like all humans lucky enough to be engaged in interesting work, have within them all the motivation they will ever need to stay in the profession and engage in the hard graft necessary to keep climbing their learning curves. What stands in their way is not a lack of financial incentives, but a working environment that all too often inhibits their natural motivation to learn and develop as professionals. It is natural for headteachers to fear complacency in their staff, but the very things that some heads instinctively do because of this fear, ultimately holds many teachers back.

We recognise that balance is needed here. There are a minority of teachers who are unlikely to develop this intrinsic motivation, regardless of how carefully school leadership nurtures their working environment. For this minority, using performance-related pay as a form of controlled motivation might well work. However, it comes at the cost of undermining the majority of teachers' natural inclination to improve. As Luke's story illustrates, it is more likely to be part of the problem than part of the solution. Autonomous motivation, by contrast, is the ultimate sustainable resource: widespread, freely available and infinitely replenishable. Teachers usually contain within them all the energy they need to keep growing, if only we can stop isolating, denigrating and micro-managing them. Of course, trust alone is not enough for most to find a way to get better at teaching. In the next chapter, we will describe the complex process of supporting teachers in getting better at their jobs.

Things that schools can do without waiting for policymakers

- Teachers need a sense of autonomy, but this does not mean leaving teachers free to do things that undermine collective organisational structures or pupil learning. As a first step, encourage every teacher to set his or her own performance targets for the coming year. The role of school leaders is to support teachers in crafting plans that really will improve their practice. The next chapter provides some ideas to help experienced teachers develop further.

- Teachers want to feel they are getting better at their job. Create multiple, low-stakes approaches to helping them measure improvements in their practice, whether this is through developing tests and quizzes to monitor pupil learning or lesson observations to watch how a specific technique they are trying out is developing.

- Most teachers enjoy working and learning alongside others and find it helps them achieve their goals. Be flexible about who these 'others' are. Create channels – whether through development sessions or noticeboards – for teachers with similar goals to find each other in the school. Seek out the local events or forums to make connections across schools. If any of your teachers choose to attend a TeachMeet or conference in their personal time, give them a 3-minute platform to tell others about it, both to celebrate the commitment they have made and to let others know what is out there.

- Review your performance-related pay policy. Remove targets that are based on things that are partly outside the control of a teacher, such as GCSE grades. Link performance appraisal specifically to an agreed professional development plan, where the teacher commits to improving their practice and the school commits to giving them the time and space to learn. Make it clear that teachers in your school are not competing with each other and that it is possible for all teachers to succeed in meeting their goals.

- Recognise your own fallibility in making judgments about other teachers. We pointed out in Chapter 4 that headteachers do know quite a lot about the quality of their own teachers, but they acquire this through slow accumulation of soft evidence. We now know that our capacity to judge high quality teaching in a lesson observation is rather limited and is affected by classroom pupil composition.[149] We also know that pupil test scores do not cleanly capture teacher quality.[150] Do not place too much weight on any single measure of a teacher's performance.

CHAPTER SIX

Teacher development
Habits, coaches and caves

In Chapter 2 we saw how experience acts as a powerful performance enhancer for early-career teachers. We also saw how the rate at which teachers learn – the steepness of their learning curves – can be increased by giving them a supportive working environment, and providing them with stable teaching assignments that allow them to master the specific skills associated with teaching a particular subject or year group. So far, so positive. But teacher learning curves have attracted most attention not for the progress they reveal in the early years, but for the way they flatten off thereafter. Most of us would expect to keep getting better at our jobs throughout our careers, or at least for the first couple of decades. But the data shows that the typical teacher seems to stop improving far sooner. Indeed, in 2009 the world's richest man gave a talk in Long Beach, California, called *Mosquitos, malaria and education,* in which he argued that the plateau in the learning curve is among the most important unsolved public policy problems the world faces. Soon afterwards, the Bill and Melinda Gates Foundation announced one third of a billion dollars ($335,000,000) of investment for research and development to tackle it.[151] It is easy to see why Gates is captivated by this problem. Why *does* the performance enhancer suddenly stop working?

To understand how learning from experience malfunctions, we first need to look at how it functions. Researchers have been studying how people acquire expertise through experience for well over a century now, stretching back at least as far as Bryan and Harter's pioneering study on the skills of Morse Code operators.[152] Time and again, studies have documented the necessity of practice for acquiring expertise in a range of disciplines including music, mathematics, tennis and swimming. [153] But the very same studies also showed that extra practice sometimes got people nowhere at all. This left a puzzle for researchers who needed to explain how practice can be necessary for acquiring skill, but at the same time be insufficient. In an attempt to square these findings, Anders Ericsson and colleagues reviewed the literature on skills acquisition and developed the concept of deliberate practice. Paring it down to its essentials, deliberate practice requires that an individual:[154]

1   does a well-defined task with a focus on improving a specific aspect of performance;
2   gets feedback on how they performed;
3   repeats the task, adjusting their practice in light of the feedback.

To test this theory, the researchers worked with the violinists at the elite Music Academy of West Berlin.[155] They asked the professors at the school to nominate violinists falling into three groups: the very best students in the academy, the good students and the least good. The violinists were asked to keep detailed diaries recording the type and duration of practice in which they engaged and also generated retrospective estimates of accumulated hours of practice over their musical careers. The researchers then looked at the relationship between the amount of practice, the type of practice and the skill of the musicians. Their findings supported the framework above: while the very best and the middle tier violinists had accumulated a broadly equivalent amount of time practising (gaining experience), the way in which the very best violinists practised corresponded more closely to the model of deliberate practice. Their study could therefore explain the experience paradox by showing that people only learn from *certain types* of experience, i.e. those that have the form of deliberate practice.

The Music Academy findings in this specific domain have been replicated in a range of areas from chess[156], to piano[157], to typing[158]. As these empirical findings have accumulated, a consensus has developed that deliberate practice is a key component of how people acquire expertise.[159] Even the most sophisticated critics of deliberate practice regard it as a necessary (though not sufficient) condition for acquiring skill.[160] On their own, these studies are of questionable relevance to how teachers acquire expertise. Recent research, however, has replicated these empirical findings in public service settings, particularly in medicine, which has the best available data. Researchers have found that expertise is positively associated with deliberate practice for doctors[161], nurses[162] and surgeons[163]; while having little discernible relationship with the raw amount of time on the job. Another useful feature of medicine for studying deliberate practice is the increasing use of simulation-based training. This can be formulated to either resemble or not resemble deliberate practice, allowing a direct test of the theory. For example, one research team conducted a randomised controlled trial to study the effect of simulator training on surgical performance and found that those who took part in additional deliberate-practice type training exercises performed the surgery quicker and more accurately.[164] Indeed, a recent meta-analysis of fourteen studies using simulated deliberate practice found that this method "is superior to traditional clinical medical education in achieving specific clinical skill acquisition goals."[165]

Deliberate practice provides an empirically-supported framework for understanding how people acquire expertise in a range of domains. Conversely, it can also help us to think about why learning curves level off. Teachers will cease to gain additional expertise if they: stop practising, stop getting useful feedback about their practise, or stop adjusting their practise in light of this feedback. We have seen in previous chapters why so many teachers leave the classroom and cease to practise the craft of teaching. But why would a teacher who remains in the classroom suddenly cease to acquire useful feedback, or fail to adjust their practise in light of it?

* * *

Let's start by looking at feedback. Teachers make hundreds of instructional choices, whether consciously or unconsciously, every day in the classroom. Is the class ready to be introduced to counting in fives or should we repeat counting in tens? I can see four children are getting restless and distracted, so is it time to bring the quiet writing exercise to a close for the whole class? Will it distress Jonny if I ask him to answer this question that he almost certainly doesn't know the answer to, or will it re-engage him from looking out the window? Teachers *must* make these choices, yet it is hard for them to find out whether the choices made improved learning or not.

Perhaps the most important reason for this is that feedback is often inadequate, ambiguous or misleading, making it hard to ascertain whether what they did actually worked. The problem here is that we can only infer learning – the long-term retention and transfer of knowledge and skills – from performance.[166] Performance is the thing we can see and measure. Learning, by contrast, takes place inside students' heads and is unobservable. One often deviates substantially from the other. For example, when Becky was learning to play the recorder as a child, her mum felt pleased with the progress she had made in reading music. It was only when they switched to a new book by a different publisher, however, that it became clear that Becky was looking at the position of the top of the note's stick on the stave, rather than the placement of the note's dot! The performance concealed the lack of learning, and so Becky had to start-over in learning to interpret the sheet music.

Divergence between performance and learning is a pervasive problem in classrooms. Professor Rob Coe has argued that much that goes on in the classroom – students busy doing lots of work in a calm environment, appearing engaged, being given feedback and (usually) supplying correct answers – can be poor proxies for the amount of learning that is taking place.[167] This is particularly true in cases where pupils like a certain teaching technique, and therefore respond positively to it, but the technique does not actually bring about much learning. Dylan Wiliam has also argued persuasively that the canonical method of checking understanding – asking for hands up – is highly flawed on the grounds that the teacher only collects information from one partly-self-selecting child among all those in the class.[168]

The Gates Foundation's huge research investment has recently produced important scientific evidence on this point. Their researchers trained practising teachers to observe lessons and rate the quality of teaching and learning. These observers were party to the same information as the teachers taking the lesson: they observed the teaching methods used, the set of pupil responses to questions, the amount of time pupils spent on-task, the extent of misbehaviour, and so on. Yet, the Gates Foundation researchers found that if one teacher-observer gave a lesson a top grade, then there was a 78 per cent chance that a second teacher-observer gave it a lower grade. Similarly, if a lesson was given a bottom grade, then there was a 90 per cent chance a second teacher-observer gave it a higher grade.[169] Two teachers watching the same classroom can therefore come to very different conclusions about the amount of learning occurring. Michael Strong, from the University of California, has also investigated whether teachers can accurately judge the amount of learning that is occurring from what they see in a lesson. [170] His research team identified teachers whose pupils made high progress three years in a row, and teachers whose pupils made low progress three years in a row, and filmed their lessons. The researchers then asked a separate group of teachers and school leaders to watch clips from these videos and categorise them as either low or high progress teachers. They found that the observer-teachers did no better than a random coin flip at categorising the teachers correctly.

This problem of missing feedback from instructional choices helps explain why the learning curves of experienced teachers level off. Early in a teacher's career, there are plenty of opportunities to acquire useful feedback. For example, many trainee and recently qualified teachers have access to good classroom observation and mentoring. Moreover, in the early stages of a teachers' careers, poor instructional choices often provide immediate and visible feedback. Some things very obviously do not work and, once an early-career teacher has watched a lesson descend into chaos after trying to use a particular technique, they will likely have the incident burned into their memory. This helps inexperienced teachers improve quite quickly.

Once the low hanging fruit have been harvested, however, more nuanced judgements are needed. If the students don't have an adverse reaction to two possible teaching approaches, tending to stay calm and apparently engaged in response to both, then working out which of two options leads to more learning is very difficult. Of course, skilled teachers can and do use sophisticated techniques to assess the learning that has occurred in a lesson or over a term. But even when they do get an accurate read out, it is necessary to judge whether teaching the lesson another way would have been better or worse, and that is an altogether more challenging prospect. Future situations may present themselves to test an alternative, but there will likely be subtle differences. Jonny might be re-engaged by asking him the stretching questions, but Jenny may not. Understanding the impact of specific instructional choices, many hundreds of which make up each lesson, is even harder. The consequence is that, even when teachers are working very hard and diligently collecting evidence on pupil learning to the best of their ability, useful feedback becomes more and more difficult to acquire.

*   *   *

The deliberate practice framework suggests that, even if feedback is available, experience can cease contributing to expertise when teachers no longer adjust their practice in response to the feedback. Dylan Wiliam gives the example of research by Mary Rowe (1986) which shows that, if teachers wait two or three seconds after asking a question before accepting a response, then pupils learn more.[171] According to Wiliam, this research was widely publicised, well known, but not generally acted upon by teachers. This finding demands explanation, particularly since all that teachers had to do to incorporate the findings into their practice was wait around for a while longer before doing any more teaching! Wiliam suggests that habits are an important reason that teachers' question-asking practices proved so resistant to change. Psychological research provides ample support for this point. Thomas Webb from the University of Manchester and Pascal Sheeran from the University of Sheffield reviewed 47 experimental studies looking at whether people translate their intentions (e.g. aiming to deploy Rowe's wait-time research in class) into actions (e.g. actually waiting longer after asking questions), and found only a weak link between the two.[172] When they interrogated the data further, they found that the most important reason that people fail to follow through on their intentions is habit: automatic behaviours that are cued by our environment. Research suggests that humans are particularly prone to forming habits if they work in stable (unchanging) environments, if they perform the same actions many times, or if they work under stress.[173] Teaching ticks all these boxes. One classroom looks much the same as the next, cuing the same techniques. Certain aspects of teaching are also very repetitive: Wiliam estimates that by the time teachers have spent ten years in the classroom they will have asked around a quarter of a million questions![174] And we all know, either from experience, or from hard data, that teaching is often a highly stress-ful job.[175]

It is therefore unsurprising that teachers develop habits, which prove difficult to shift, even in the light of compelling feedback that the habitual behaviours should be replaced. Indeed, neuroscientists define habitual behaviour partly on the basis that it is "insensitive to reinforcer devaluation," that is, immune to feedback.[176] To be clear, this is not a criticism of teachers: learning curves have been shown to flatten off in professions from insurance sales to air traffic controllers.[177] Rather, habits are just a basic part of human psych-ology. It is also important to point out that, just as with restrictions in feedback, the establishment of habits is itself the direct result of previous learning. As we saw in Chapter 2 with surgeons and our cha-cha dancer, it is essential that the behaviours we learn become automatic in order to free up bandwidth in working memory to concentrate on acquiring the next layer of a skill. Learning curves therefore flatten off, in part, because the potential for new learning gets crushed under the weight of past learning, which has crystallized into automatic behaviour. Establishing habits is therefore simul-taneously the aim and the enemy of acquiring new expertise. This point was not lost on Bryan and Harter, who wrote in their 1899 study of expertise development among Morse Code operatives: "In the measure that he has mastered the occupation, it has mastered him. Body and soul, from head to foot he has, or one may say he *is* – the array of habits which constitutes proficiency."[178]

*   *   *

When I ask Kate Forbes about teachers' learning curves flattening off after five or so years in the classroom, she pauses for a minute, and then shoots me a wry smile:

> Teachers reach the sort of, 'Year 8': You're not new, you haven't just come from primary. But you're not in a GCSE year. You've got no accountability, you're not special, and you're getting alright lesson observations and things are going OK. It's perpetual year 8.

Having trained as a teacher in 2004, and then qualified as an Advanced Skills Teacher, she speaks from personal experience.

> My teaching was good, but it wasn't getting better. I was definitely being challenged, physically, emotionally, day to day: someone phones in sick and you've got to figure out who is teaching year 8; somebody's crying in the corridor and you've got to sort them out. You are constantly on your toes. But I wasn't being challenged academically or professionally. I wasn't progressing as a teacher.

I have come to Swanage in Dorset to interview Kate because, frustrated with her own plateau, she decided to take a sabbatical from teaching to set up an experiment aimed at reshaping professional development, and helping teachers keep moving up their learning curves. She has a shock of short, bright blond hair and speaks rapidly as she describes the 'tuning cycle' she has been working on with fifteen other teachers.

Tuning cycles identify a specific aspect of teaching practice and bring together a group of teachers to iteratively refine this one technique over the course of a term. Kate's three groups, clustered by subject, chose to focus their tuning cycle on exit tickets: short, no-stakes quizzes, done by all pupils at the end of a lesson; used by teachers to assess learning and plan future instruction.[179] Each group of participants would meet for 90 minutes each fortnight and take it in turns to talk through the current iteration of their exit tickets, report on how they used it in the last fortnight, and then receive feedback from the other participants. The participants would then write up what they had learned from the critique and how they would adapt their exit ticket for use in their classrooms during the next two-week cycle. The Fellow assigned to each group would help keep the meeting on track, offer expert feedback, and ensure the feedback and criticism from others was detailed enough to prompt real reflection. The objective was for the teachers in each group to collectively hone and refine the exit ticket technique through multiple rounds of feedback and adaptation over the course of a term. Kate proudly shows me the fortnight-by-fortnight development of the exit tickets on her laptop, tracking the changes that were made by each teacher. "You could see them get better," she says, beaming.

When Kate finishes describing the process, I ask her how this differs from the type of professional development she had been receiving during her own plateau. Her response comes quickly:

> With normal CPD, you go to the session, you take away a technique from it, which you want to try, you maybe do it once or twice in your classroom, but then perhaps it doesn't work so well or you get distracted by day-to-day stuff, and then you kind of find it in a dusty folder in your desk at the end of the summer term.

When I ask her why tuning cycles should be any different, she begins by pointing to the voluntary nature of the whole exercise:

> The impetus was on them . . . None of them were doing it to get a promotion or get a pay rise or whatever. They just wanted to develop a little bit of their practice and do something different. We were not in contact with their Principals or in contact with their line managers. They were doing it because they wanted to.

Kate's insight fits squarely with what the psychology literature, including Self Determination Theory, tells us about the importance of autonomous motivation in changing behaviour, from exercising more to working harder at school.[180]

Kate is also keen to highlight the power of the participants' mutual commitments to making specific changes to their practice. "Other people were giving you their time. You knew that everybody was waiting there online for you. There's no way you couldn't submit your exit ticket, because people would just be sitting there during their evening, waiting." Meta-analysis has indeed shown that committing to something in front of others is also among the most powerful ways of changing deeply engrained, habitual behaviours.[181] Kate is clear on this point. "If nobody is following up, checking, critiquing, nobody is going to do any long term thinking." But the critical thing for Kate is that:

> It really was a tuning cycle, with constant tuning. I did an education masters in Leadership and Management for Learning . . . every so often I would have to get an assignment in, and I would stay up late and do it. I did a really good dissertation on the tokenistic use of Student View in schools. But I never did anything with it. It has never impacted my practice. It never touched the classroom. But with tuning cycles, it is embedded. For example, when one teacher's student, Dan, responded badly to it in the last cycle, next time we could ask "How did Dan respond this time?" It's that constant tuning with feedback that you don't get with traditional CPD.

Kate's tuning cycle is interesting because it represents a radical new approach to CPD, led by teachers who were fed up with getting nowhere with standard professional development. While there has not yet been a formal evaluation of the tuning cycle approach, it is supported by what psychology and economics tells us about how and when people learn. By focusing and pooling their learning around a single, tightly defined technique, and by drawing on the expert feedback from the Fellow, the tuning cycle participants were able to gather far more feedback than they would have done through solo implementation of the technique in their own classes, relying purely on the reactions of their students to assess the effectiveness of their approach. By increasing the speed with which people learn from experience, and committing to a term-long effort to hone a particular technique, tuning cycle participants are also more likely to persist through the difficult early efforts at implementing and developing the skills necessary to deploy a technique effectively.[182] Tuning cycles bear some resemblance to other group-based professional development programmes, such as Teacher Learning Communities and Lesson Study, but it is distinctive in the emphasis it places on expert feedback from the Fellow.[183] Kate was crystal clear on this point: "They all said the feedback from the Fellow was critical. They were desperate for that individualised feedback."

Kate's tuning cycle is a coaching intervention, in that it involves sustained practice of specific teaching techniques, with individualised feedback.[184] It is also very clearly a case of deliberate practice. There has been an explosion of rigorous research on coaching interventions in the last few years. Indeed, a 2017 meta-analysis found 44 rigorous studies evaluating such programmes, including 40 randomised controlled trials.[185] Contrary to Kate's description of the average CPD ending up in a "dusty folder in your desk at the end of the summer term" the meta-analysis finds that coaching interventions caused measurable changes in teaching practice with an average effect size of 0.58, conventionally considered to be a "large" effect. These results are supported by meta-analysis of interventions outside of teaching which also show coaching to be a powerful driver of behaviour change, particularly when it is autonomy supportive.[186] Kate's explanation for why her tuning cycle seemed to change behaviour in a way that most CPD does not is therefore closely aligned with what the research tells us.

The meta-analysis also shows that these changes in teaching practice fed through to improved pupil attainment. Indeed, it showed a strong correlation (0.64) between the two: the more that a coaching intervention changed teacher practice, the larger the impact on pupil attainment. The average effect size of coaching interventions on pupil attainment is 0.15, which is equivalent to about two months' additional progress per pupil, according to the Educational Endowment Foundation.[187] It is worth stressing here that these are not the results of one or two outstanding, highly-funded studies, conducted under ideal conditions. Rather, this is the *average* effect sizes across all teacher coaching studies that have ever been rigorously evaluated.

One coaching model which stands out is the My Teaching Partner Secondary (MTPS). This is the result of over a decade of careful research and development by educational psychologists at the University of Virginia in the US. MTPS is a year-long professional development programme to improve teachers' interactions with pupils and improve pupils' motivation and effort at school. The intervention is based on the CLASS scoring system, which describes a specific set of skills or behaviours for teachers to master and has been shown to predict student achievement gains.[188] Participating teachers attend an initial workshop in which the framework is explained and are provided with an annotated video library illustrating effective use of the behaviours. Teachers then practise using these in their classrooms and record videos of their work, which are then sent to an expert coach via the internet. After the coach has reviewed the video, they provide feedback to the participant via phone. As in all coaching interventions, the coaches work *with* the coachee to ensure they deploy and develop the practices in a way that suits them – and then hold them to account for the progress against this. The fortnightly cycle of practice, feedback and refinement – a textbook example of deliberate practice – continues for one year. The intervention has now been tested in two separate randomised controlled trials, which both found near identical impacts on attainment, amounting to an effect size of around 0.2.[189]

*   *   *

We started this chapter by asking: why do learning curves flatten off? We have come some way in developing our explanation, so it's worth summarising our answer before ending the chapter. In the early stages of a teacher's career, it is easy to learn from experience, because it is quite easy to spot what really does or doesn't work. However, as teachers adjust their practice in response to these early lessons learned, two things happen. First, teachers begin to exhaust the low-hanging fruit of accurate, unambiguous feedback, requiring them to make ever-more difficult distinctions between the amounts of learning that result from alternative instructional choices. Second, as they develop a repertoire of reasonably effective teaching techniques, this practice becomes consolidated in long term memory and in doing so becomes automated, and therefore insensitive to feedback. In both cases, the potential for learning from experience gets smothered by the accumulated weight of past learning. *Continuing professional development is therefore harder than initial teacher training in important ways.* Nevertheless, a wave of recent research on coaching interventions shows that they can reliably foster changes in practice and keep teachers moving up their learning curve late into their careers. The evidence we have reviewed in this chapter suggests that coaching is highly effective because it combines, in one intervention, the method of improvement – deliberate practice – with the necessary inducements to improve – autonomy and committing to change in front of others. Coaching therefore gives teachers both the means and the motive to continue their ascent up their learning curves.

Learning from experience is like trying to navigate through a long, dark cave. At first, teachers can navigate using the light that penetrates into the cave from the entrance and, despite the difficult terrain, progress is swift. The further they progress, however, the more the light fades and the harder it is to find the way ahead. In the absence of good information about whether they are heading in the right direction, our intrepid teachers tend to employ the same techniques that worked during the early stages of the journey. If it helped them progress then, it should be a reasonable bet now. And when picking their way between the rocks in low light, using the steps that worked for them in the past seems like the safe, prudent thing to do. But in the absence of any light, it is perhaps no wonder that most teachers end up failing to make much progress. Coaching is like a torch, illuminating a very specific route forward. By showing the way, it helps teachers make progress one step at a time. And by illuminating the destination, helps show how much further teachers can go with the right support.

Things that schools can do without waiting for policymakers

- Run an audit to quantify how much of the CPD in your schools involves deliberate practice, autonomy support and accountability from colleagues for making progress. Deans for Impact have developed 16 questions you can ask yourself to determine whether the CPD in your school involves deliberate practice.[190]

- Where CPD contains none of the characteristics of deliberate practice, consider stopping it. Invest the resources you save in developing more CPD that does have the characteristics of deliberate practice.

- If you don't currently have any trained coaches in your school, consider buying in coaching support. Shop around to see if you can find a programme such as MTPS which has been shown to improve attainment in rigorous experimental evaluations.

- If budgets are tight, consider setting up your own tuning cycle groups for teachers who are keen to develop a specific aspect of their practice. Remember to focus on specific aspects of practice over a sustained period. Invest time ensuring that participants feel comfortable offering each other honest, constructive feedback.

- In addition, consider developing your own in-house coaching expertise, which can provide a sustainable resource for improving teaching. Anthony Grant from the University of Sydney has written about how to go about embedding coaching in your organisation.[191]

CHAPTER SEVEN

Teacher workload
Auditing the hamster wheel

Lucy Perry is exhausted. That is why she is sitting in our offices one summer term, hoping to throw away six years of training and experience to answer our phones and manage our diaries. The pressure of being a year six teacher, whose children are the first to be judged on the new National Curriculum tests, is too much to bear. "I'm not a novice at this," she says, "but I cannot see how I am supposed to get 85 per cent of my class to meet expectations, as my headteacher expects me to."

The job has become impossible in her eyes, but Lucy Perry has not yet given up. Far from it. She works every day, every evening and every weekend.

> The planning and the marking burdens that my headteacher places on me are huge. If I plan one literacy lesson then that means differentiating the work in many ways to allow each child to access it. But marking is the bigger deal because every time they produce something then you are expected to mark it in different colour pens. Then the children respond to that feedback and then we respond again giving them 'next steps', and so on. Their books have to look like this masterpiece of colour for every piece of work. And this is for six lessons a day. Every day for 30 children. So teaching is actually quite a small part of my job.

Lucy's school may be at one end of the tail of over-the-top demands but many parts of her experience will resonate with teachers across the country. The workload demands extend far beyond planning and marking. "We write reports three times a year, have a continuous schedule of assessments", Lucy explains.

> And each time the students are tested, I am expected to mark it that night, take the data and input it into our management system. I am in a hamster wheel with SLT constantly saying to me: 'do this, do this, I want this, I want this now.'

Markbooks have moved from teachers' bags to centralised systems. In a survey of over a 1,000 teachers, who were asked how often they were required to centrally deposit data with the senior leadership team, 80 per cent reported they did it at least termly, well over half said it was at least half-termly and almost 1-in-10 said it was more frequently than half-termly.[192] As a teacher 15 years ago, Becky was never asked to do this once.

All teachers are busy people. So busy that it is almost impossible to get them to find time to respond to an online survey. And yet, the strength of feeling about the teacher workload problem is such that at the end of 2014, 32,832 of them found the time to respond to the government's Workload Challenge consultation.[193] Teachers in England reported that they were working between 55 and 59 hours per week on average, with school leaders working considerably more.[194] Just over 10 per cent of these working hours were at evenings or at weekends. Yet less than half this time – about 20 hours – is spent in the classroom with students. Those who work in other professional jobs may (correctly) remark that 59 hours per week, with longer holidays to compensate, is quite similar to other professions.[195] But this does not take into account the intensity and performance involved in teaching – we wouldn't expect an actor to be on stage for five hours a day, five days a week and 39 weeks a year.[196]

This is not the first time there have been concerns about workload in the teaching profession. When Becky first entered the classroom back in 2003, there was a poster in the staffroom, produced by the Government and (most of) the unions, with a list of things that teachers must not do: photocopying, processing forms for school trips, and so on. Estelle Morris, then Secretary of State, said:

> A tired teacher is not an effective teacher. Nor is that teacher allowed to focus on what is most important – teaching. Teachers, on average, are expected to spend some 20 per cent of their time on non-teaching tasks that other adults could do just as well instead.[197]

Teachers today would likely jump at the chance to spend just 20 per cent of their time on non-teaching tasks. Teachers *have* been given greater non-contact time, which takes them out of the classroom and lowers the burden of covering for absent colleagues, but it has been overwhelmed by the raft of bureaucratic activities that we see Lucy Perry carries out each week. This is why (self-reported) working hours have risen by around five hours a week in the past five years.[198,199] Teachers overwhelmingly report that the level of detail, duplication or bureaucracy in their job is unnecessary or unproductive. They most frequently complain about how they are asked to record, input, monitor and analyse data (56 per cent) and about excessive marking expectations (53 per cent).[200]

For a teacher from the past, like Becky, this bureaucracy appears to be the defining feature of teaching today. Teaching may still take place in private in a classroom; learning may still take place inside a child's mind, where it is hard to see. However, teaching is no longer a private endeavour. Schools have fallen victim to an audit culture in which teachers feel obliged to create a paper trail that proves to people not present at the time that unwritten activities really happened.

*   *   *

If you asked a headteacher why they were trying to audit teaching and learning in their school they'd probably give you one of three answers: Assessment for Learning; the need for centralised monitoring of pupils; or teacher performance management. The Assessment for Learning argument contends that managers, through centralising and standardising data, assessment and marking systems, are helping teachers use data for pupil feedback and to inform teaching. [201] This argument presumes that it is optimal for heads to override discretion on the part of teachers, even though teaching and assessing necessarily needs to take different forms in different subjects. Marking policy restrictions that are mandated along similar lines are causing teachers to spend hours longer on marking each week than they would if they were left to choose how to give feedback to pupils.[202] Professor Dylan Wiliam – one of the architects of Assessment for Learning – said that if you price teachers' time appropriately, in England we spend about two and a half billion pounds a year on feedback and it has almost no effect on student achievement.[203] He describes marking as the most expensive public relations exercise in history, though for an auditor it conveniently makes marks on paper, of course.

The second argument school leaders might make is that they need to see the pupil data to action school-wide approaches to supporting a child. Technology creates the illusion that a headteacher can meaningfully analyse 15,000 data points on pupil progress during the October half-term (that's just one point per pupil per subject in a typically-sized secondary school). It is simply impossible for a human-being to do this. Let's pretend for a moment that this data is meaningful and does reflect true learning taking place in a school. What then is it realistic for headteachers to do with it? At best, headteachers will take rough class averages and identify outlier classes, which begs the question why they didn't just ask for the class average in the first place. They might also be realistically able to act on a list of two-dozen students who are experiencing significant difficulties across all subjects – a list that could have been compiled in minutes by asking teachers to jot down the names of pupils causing concern on a list in the staffroom.

The final claimed purpose of all this data is to monitor teacher and departmental performance, a theme we touched on in Chapter 5. This is, perhaps, more understandable if we recall that the rise of the audit culture took place in an era in which even *very* bad teachers didn't lose their jobs. The trouble is, this audit culture is unhelpful to almost everyone in organisations that rely on professional autonomy, as schools do. This point is eloquently made in a famous presentation by the CEO of Netflix, Reed Hastings, and his colleague Patty McCord. [204]

In their view, bureaucracy and audit cultures don't work for those workers who are weak and lack the capacity to improve – if we can't help them get better then these people just need to leave teaching. They also say audit cultures don't work for those workers who are poor and don't care – these people also need to leave teaching. Sure, the pupil-progress paper trail provides the very detailed evidence-base that leaders needed to go through the long, draining "capability procedures" necessary to manage them out. However, by forcing all teachers to adhere to this paper trail they are causing untold collateral damage to great teachers' lives in the process.

They aren't necessary for those workers who are talented and well-motivated. Rather, they only work for the small subset of people who are a little lazy and unfocused, but who with the right hard-edged accountability system will get stuck into their job and improve what they do. We train our school leaders to implement an audit culture that is probably raising the standards of a tiny percentage of teachers by forcing them to demonstrate the work they are putting in. But for the most part, this enormous 'effort' ends up coming from the good teachers – who were always good at teaching – but who are now forced to plough their energy into generating audit trails necessary to bounce the tiny of number of lazy teachers into work and to help generate the audit trail necessary to support the capability process for the weakest.

*   *   *

The results of this audit culture on teacher happiness are clear. Over half of teachers say they are dissatisfied with the hours they work each week. Around 60 per cent say they are unhappy with the balance between their professional and personal commitments.[205]

The problem is not simply the long hours' culture in teaching in England, for long hours are reported in teaching professions in some other countries too.[206] However, in many of these countries it is not associated with feelings of work overload and stagnating pupil standards.[207]

Equally, many teachers in England choose to spend their evenings blogging and their weekends going to conferences because teaching is their hobby as well as their job. As we saw in Chapter 5, when teachers invest considerable efforts due to autonomous motivations, those efforts are accompanied by feelings of vitality and energy, whereas teachers' efforts due to controlled motivations are accompanied by a sense of being drained and exhausted.[208] Our problem is that surveys report that teachers in England perceive a lack of control and ownership over their work, undertaking many tasks, particularly documentation, which are not seen as supporting learning.[209] It is this, and not simply the longer hours, that results in a sense of being drained and exhausted. Lucy Perry doesn't feel like she has any autonomy – she is trapped on the bureaucracy hamster wheel. And she isn't the only one. Indeed, dissatisfaction with workload has now become such a crisis that the Government and unions have made another workload poster![210]

* * *

Explaining the teacher workload phenomenon means explaining why thousands of schools, operating seemingly independently, have chosen to embark on a similar set of bureaucratic activities that were never mandated and cannot be explained by any sort of efficient drive to improve pupil learning. Economics is good at explaining why profit-driven organisations will choose to pursue identical strategies, arguing that over time they will all converge on the most efficient forms of technology and ways of organising production. Those that do not will be weeded out by the strictures of the market. But trying to explain why many organisations pursue identical yet inefficient strategies is a little more difficult. For an explanation, we turn instead to sociology.

In 1983, Paul DiMaggio and Walter Powell published an article that describes how this phenomenon of institutional isomorphism – processes that make organisations evolve (morph) to become more similar (iso) – came about.[211] It seems perfectly suited to describing the English schooling system today, where similar (and yet inefficient) practices have driven up workload without any gains in educational standards. They describe three processes that can take place in industries that cause institutions to become more alike.

The first they call 'coercive isomorphism', whereby political influences and the problem of legitimacy forces institutions to conform. It is this force that is on the tip of almost every teacher's tongue when you ask them who is to blame for the workload crisis: Ofsted. [212] It is certainly Ofsted who Lucy primarily blames for her enormous workload. "There is so much work I could pinpoint over the past seven years that was just done for Ofsted and has since gone in the bin because it hasn't been needed. It was always just-in-case," she explains. And yet what is amazing about her response is that in Lucy's entire teaching career she has never been inspected. Her school was judged as outstanding in 2008 and so, provided its data remains high and parents don't complain, it will not be inspected again. This doesn't seem to reduce the terror that the threat of an inspection has on her school's management team:

> So much of what I do every day is about how we look. How we look when Ofsted come in. How we look to parents and others who visit our school. So the displays have to look good and the books have to look lovely. Everything has to look just right, without regard for what is happening to the children on a day-to-day basis. In our school we can always pull out a book or pull up the data and show how amazing we are.

Ofsted and the threat of the inspection, with particular preconceived ideas about what constitutes "good" teaching and leadership, is a prime example of a coercive isomorphic force. The reason that Lucy has to mark her books in a way that leaves an auditable paper trail of 'progress' is, in part, because Ofsted implicitly incentivises such behaviour. Local authority and multi-academy trust systems of monitoring, which often expect 'data drops' of a particular frequency and format, also force schools to herd toward certain workload-inducing behaviours. Each data drop generates its own sequence of assessments and preparations for assessments in order to satisfy the demands from on high. In each of these cases, the political decision-makers – the inspectorate or middle-tier advisors – do not directly experience the consequences of the demands they place on teachers, which leads to poor trade-offs being made and workload spiralling out of control.

What is strange about this coercive force is that Ofsted claim they didn't mean for this auditable trail of teaching activities to be created. Even if they did mean it once, it is clear that they regret it and want it to go away. Not all school inspection systems generate the need for paperwork. In England, one turning point appears to have taken place around 2005 when long inspections with large teams were replaced with smaller and shorter inspections. Where once the inspection team's job was to spend a week unearthing evidence on school practice, now the inspection is so fleetingly short that all inspectors can really do is check the headteacher has sufficient written evidence to support their own self-evaluation form. Headteachers therefore developed a cascade of school policies – on curriculum, assessment, marking and so on – to mirror what they thought Ofsted would be looking for. In their new role as headteacher-cum-inspector, they now required teachers to submit their planning, marking and assessment data – data that was once largely private.

It is far too simplistic, and arguably incorrect, to say that managerialism arose through the explicitly mandated coercive policies of Ofsted. The second force driving organisations to become more similar is that of mimetic isomorphism, or mimicking behaviour. Organisations across most industries frequently copy each other's good ideas, but what makes schools unusual is that unhelpful ideas frequently spread.

DiMaggio and Powell contend that unhelpful institutional mimicry happens through lack of information and understanding. In our case, we do not fully understand how school operations lead to improvements in children's learning. One consequence of this is that an inspector could ask a headteacher *anything* or hold *any* number of views on the activities and documentation they expect to see in a school. The safest response to uncertainty around 'what Ofsted wants' is simply to mimic the behaviours of other schools. Mimicking, as much as anything, led to headteachers purchasing the now ubiquitous pupil tracking systems. Uncertainty about how to measure pupil progress after the government removed levels led to them employing marking and assessment consultants to help them standardise school practice. Schools rightly choose to act as sheep because even if the herd makes the wrong decision about which way to run, it is still safer to be nestled in the middle of it.

In this interplay between coercive and mimetic forces, Ofsted does not invent and then mandate practices that increase workload. Instead, having seen these managerial practices arise somewhere in the system, they latch onto them and encourage other schools to copy them through the industry of 'Mocksteds' and the now-abandoned case studies.[213] And the reason they did this for auditing policies more than others is that they fixed Ofsted's difficulty that they no longer have the resources to actually learn about school practices through a long inspection.

DiMaggio and Powell would argue that there is one final pressure that drives schools to act similarly, rather than to pursue distinct identities, and we think this force is critical to understanding the *perpetuation* of the workload crisis in teaching. They call this force 'normative isomorphism' and describe it as the collective struggle of members of an occupation to define the conditions and methods of their work, to control entry to the profession and to legitimise their autonomy as professionals.[214] For many teachers, their professional identity is bound up with the idea that their methods must be personalised to every child and that they must plan every lesson they do, in their own way, and in their own style. This generates an enormous amount of additional workload. Those who conform with the prevailing ideas of what it means to *be a teacher* are more likely to become the next leaders of the profession, reinforcing this dynamic.

Another normative force has re-shaped teacher identity in recent years. The idea has developed that it is within the power of teachers, at least theoretically, to reduce educational inequalities and help all children achieve success. And because teachers could potentially do this, they therefore must do everything possible to make this happen. This moral imperative created a sort of neurotic insistence on every possible intervention, however marginal the gain, because not to do so would be to 'fail' pupils, especially those most in need.

School leadership has normative forces shaping their identity in quite different ways. Today's headteachers have cut their managerial teeth in a period in which *good* leaders are those who regularly collect evidence that standards are being met in each of their classrooms week-in, week-out. In part, they are able to this because large increases in school budgets between 2000 and 2010 facilitated the growth of large leadership teams in some schools, who were able to preside over elaborate systems of technology-supported audit.[215] Governors, parents, trades unions, professional development organisations and local authority networks all serve to reinforce these normative views of what constitutes high professional standards in teaching and leadership. Those teachers who don't want to subscribe to the audit culture find they cannot be promoted to leadership positions. I ask Lucy why teachers at her school don't just stand up to the head. "I feel those in middle leader positions are backing up the head's position, which makes it hard for the rest of us," she says.

> . . . the teachers who in the past have stood up to the head have been the ones who have gone for one reason and another. They either left of their own accord or there hasn't been a job for them next year.

DiMaggio and Powell tell us that these three forces causing schools to adopt similar-but-inefficient practices take hold because every institution is dependent on the state for funding and accreditation, because we don't have scientific evidence to tell us how best to organise and manage schools and because school survival is possible in spite of these inefficient practices. It explains why Lucy's head-teacher is asking to see weekly planning, sets marking rules, performs weekly book moderation and collects regular pupil tracking data. Her headteacher does these things because she believes Ofsted and others will judge her favourably if she does (coercive isomorphism). She does these things because she does not really know how best to ensure high standards of teaching and learning in her school, so copying other 'high performing' schools' processes seems the best response to uncertainty (mimetic isomorphism). And she does these things because she believes that the job of a headteacher is to put systems in place to be able to monitor the activities of staff and pupils to ensure that every child gets the attention they deserve and none of them fall behind (normative isomorphism).

The theory also tells us that, if we are to find schools that are attempting to buck the trends, then we will find them hidden away from professional networks and systems of monitoring. I found Stephen leading one such primary school in a leafy middle class village far from London. The community is small and stable enough that he knows all the children, many of their parents, and can describe what is going on in the life of every one of his teachers. He is a mature headteacher, close to retirement, who is unimpressed by the latest leadership thinking. His local authority has neither the money nor resources to bother him much. His pupils are affluent enough that his test scores keep Ofsted at bay.

In fact, when we met, Ofsted had recently completed their routine inspection of the school and so it was at the forefront of his mind. "We are in this false paradise at the moment because we are a year after our inspection so actually we are just getting on with enjoying our job and there isn't the pressure to do too much." I ask him to tell me about their recent inspection. "We are a 'Good' school," he says,

and to be an "Outstanding" school to be honest is not something I aspire to. Because my experience of schools that are outstanding is that they are very good at ticking boxes and they are not often focusing enough on the things they need to be doing. The inspector who visited us was an extremely bright former head herself. She knew the quality of what people do at my school and in her written report she was very kind, generous and accurate about us. But she had to work to an agenda – Ofsted is now a political organisation with a political agenda – and it was her job to carry that out rather than judge our school for what it was.

I ask him about what he refuses to do to satisfy inspectors:

We have not purchased a pupil tracking system because this whole business of tracking has become a blight on the curriculum, a blight on children's progress, a blight on teachers' lives and has created a whole industry out there that is feeding on teachers' fear. It is immoral. We maintain a straightforward view of which children are on track in reading, writing and maths. And we don't try to do anything else because it is a pretence to believe it is possible to track very single element of the National Curriculum. And trying to do so by using the STA judgement criteria leads to a curriculum that is so hopelessly narrow. If that's what they want education to be then you can have my resignation now, because I'm going.

Stephen gives his teachers as much freedom to manage their work as he dares, but even he finds it impossible to entirely shield his staff from the burden of the audit culture. What is the most challenging workload demand he places on his staff? He doesn't hesitate in replying that it is marking. "Again, it all comes down to the business of inspection," he says.

And it has been a very difficult line to walk because every inspector has been "on it" and yet it isn't obvious that it is really effective in improving learning. In the past I've had to tell my staff that you have to show you've been present because the inspectors are coming, but please, the most important thing you have is the conversation with the child in that moment.

The problem with a conversation with the child is that, after it finishes, nobody can check that it has happened. Marking leaves marks for others to monitor.

*　*　*

We have to resolve this unnecessary teacher workload crisis that nobody wants and that nobody will take responsibility for. Just as it took multiple initiatives and institutions to increase teacher workload to current levels, it will take a plethora of initiatives to undo it. Where the theory of institutional isomorphism succeeds in explaining why schools have created large bureaucratic audit mechanisms, it also points the way as to how we must solve the workload problem, and ensure it does not spiral out of control again. All we need to do is simultaneously re-purpose these coercive, mimetic and normative forces to ensure that the system holds manageable working hours in place.

The Government and Ofsted can try to pin in place a lower workload culture through 'coercion'. First, Government should legislate to ensure curriculum and assessment changes have at least four-year lead-in times, as they do in other countries, to give teachers time to prepare and to discourage politicians from trying unnecessary 'quick fixes'. Second, we should look again at replacing 'directed time' contracts that only specify maximum teaching hours, with ones that specify teachers' daily working hours like normal workers.[216] This would make explicit the opportunity cost of requests, requiring heads or Ofsted to specify what it is they would like teachers to stop doing. When the consequence of asking fifty teachers to spend an hour sitting in a staff meeting is that fifty hours of lesson planning are lost, a headteacher might feel rather differently about doing so! Third, we need to wean Ofsted off its dependence on managerialism to justify its paperwork-based fleetingly short inspections. This, in turn, will require us to reconsider whether longer inspections are needed to make accountability function better. In the meantime, if we take the view that more autonomy-supportive management practices would benefit the teaching profession, then Ofsted must train their inspectors in how to identify them. Headteachers must feel safe to report that they trust their staff to do a good job, if exam results show this trust is justified. Ofsted should also announce that they are to direct their inspectors to monitor coercive, inefficient workload and teacher turnover as part of their visit, and that high workload schools cannot be judged as good.

I ask Stephen what would happen if overnight Ofsted announce they have no expectations around marking, tracking, monitoring of standards, self-evaluation of data, and so on. He replies: "Headteachers would respond by inventing their own system because they are utterly brainwashed now. And let's be honest about it now . . . there are elements of that you wouldn't want to let go of." I ask Lucy a similar question and she replies:

> I don't know how much this really can be fixed by Ofsted. There is simply a massive lack of trust. I don't ever feel trusted that I know

my children and I know what to do for them. I feel I have to
constantly justify everything I do. I want to be able to set tests for
my children using my own professional judgement and at a time
that is right for my class as an experienced and qualified teacher.
But instead I am told "This week is test week and you will report
back to us." This lack of trust. I don't know where it comes from. I
just feel there is a huge element of control where they want to know
what is going in classrooms at all times. For every class.

These remarks serve to remind that, even if all coercive forces were
removed, the normative forces would likely keep high workload in
place. The main impetus for change now has to come from school
leaders themselves since they have been the agents through which
the audit culture has taken hold in schools. Asking headteachers to
reverse years of learnt behaviours, without any guarantees that we
can protect them from rogue inspectors, requires considerable bravery
and self-exposure on their part. They will only do this if we can help
them learn our new norms of autonomy-supportive leadership
through a number of important lessons.

First, that auditing teaching and learning is not really possible.
The links between what heads observe through auditing activities
and the quality of learning is simply unproven. A headteacher cannot
know what is going on in a classroom, unless they are there. They
need to learn to live with this uncomfortable truth and stop asking
for lesson plans, performing book scrutiny, reviewing marking and
collecting tracking data. All of which means learning to trust teachers
again.

Second, we have to persuade them that a trust culture is *necessary*
to give teachers the professional autonomy that they need to grow
and develop in an environment where we simply do not have the
tools or evidence to mandate how they should work. Relying on
teacher hunches and habits alone is not the ideal way for us to
organise learning in schools, but it is surely better than our attempts
to homogenise classroom practice and monitoring in entirely un-
evidenced ways to suit an audit culture that is demotivating and
burdensome for teachers.

It is not enough for leaders to learn about autonomy-supportive management practices; we also need to think about how we train professionals to handle this autonomy. Not all teachers can and will thrive under the trust culture. Most teachers can learn how to work effectively without undue monitoring and those that can't must be managed out to maintain a strong professional culture for everyone else. Once teacher shortages lessen, we should help these teachers find more appropriate careers.

And finally we come to those mimetic forces that cause silver bullets and managerial ideas to ripple through schools via Ofsted 'case studies', consultants' training courses, articles in education magazines, and so on. We should harness them to promote the many schools out there that are already using autonomy-supportive leadership practices and those schools who are already finding ways to materially lower teacher workload. However, the only way to guarantee that good advice is given out in the system – advice that maximises the trade-off between teacher effort and pupil learning – is to develop a decent scientific evidence base on how best to lead schools, on how best to develop and motivate teaching staff and on best classroom practice.

The march towards an improved scientific understanding of schooling and a more evidence-informed profession will of course be long and gradual. But if we can tackle the coercive and normative forces herding schools towards the high-workload culture then we can at least provide cover for educators looking to make the trip.

*   *   *

The sad thing about the current state of affairs is that, if you frame the question correctly, everybody knows what activities they should stop doing. I put the same question to Lucy and to Stephen:

> Overnight the government announces a ban on teachers being inside a school outside the hours of 8am and 4:30pm. No work can be taken home and school email cannot be read. How does pupil learning deteriorate?

Lucy loves this question. "Wow", she says.

> Part of me thinks that is terrifying and part of me thinks that might
> be a really positive thing. My children wouldn't have beautiful,
> wonderful flip charts on the whiteboard anymore because I do them
> at home. They may not get the scaffolding for the writing they get.
> There'd be a lot more thinking on my feet, just being present in the
> classroom without worrying about all the resources I'd created. I
> don't know what would happen if I stopped correcting all their
> spelling, grammar, and so on.

Stephen responds to the question with a long silence. "I'm not
sure that learning does deteriorate," he eventually concludes.

> Because arguably you would just get teachers who were more rested
> and relaxed and ready to be there in the morning. And brighter and
> more responsive to the children they have there. In the first instance
> what you would have is huge elation. Then you would have stress.
> Because you have a profession who is conditioned into a particular
> way of working and who would find it very hard to adjust.

For older teachers like Stephen, it would actually be a simple
return to the job as it was at the start of their career. Back then he
worked in a pretty challenging school without a teaching assistant
and yet he says:

> I don't recall my life being every weekend full of work, not at all. I
> used to arrive at school just after 7 and leave by 4. I didn't ever take
> anything home because I had managed to do it all within those
> hours. I went home and lived my life and saw my friends.

It is too late for us to save Lucy, who is still working out the final
weeks of her teaching career. She was supposed to leave in summer
2016 and actually had, in the sense that she had attended her own
leaving assembly and said tearful goodbyes to children and parents.
However, at ten past three the headteacher and deputy knocked on
her classroom door and begged her to stay for the first few weeks of

the Autumn Term. The only teacher to apply for her job – a Canadian who was backpacking round the world – had called to say he had changed his mind and wouldn't be coming after all. "The class didn't have anyone to stand in front of them come September," she said. "'And so I stood in. Weeks became months, months became terms, and I'm still here." But this summer she will not do it again, even though they have again failed to recruit.

> I want a life back. I'm now in my early thirties and I now just feel like I've missed a huge part of my life with my head in my laptop or a pile of books. I don't feel like the amount of effort I've put in has changed how well my kids would have done. I feel like they would have done well without all the hours I put in.

Right there in Lucy's final words is our answer – the audit culture is not there for the children. Standards did not rise. So, we can go back to that world where teachers taught, and then they went home and saw their friends and family. We can do it without compromising pupil learning.

Things that schools can do without waiting for policymakers

- It is very difficult to reduce workload by creating a long list of things you are doing and then picking a few things that you will stop. You thought all these things were important once, and it takes a huge hit to the ego to reverse decisions! Instead do the reverse, carry out the 8am to 4:30pm experiment in your own school, perhaps just for two weeks in the first instance. Observe what teachers choose to stop doing and then ask how you *know* these things are worth doing.

- Take some time to read the 'Ofsted Myths' to devise workload-saving changes to school practice that are consistent with the current Inspection Framework.[217] For example, although a school should have an assessment policy, it does not need to specify how frequently teachers should be marking books.

- In order to sustainably reduce written marking, teachers need to feel that they have enough feedback on pupil achievement to plan their lessons properly. Encourage groups of teachers to work together to learn how to carry out more efficient approaches to gaining feedback than marking books individually, such as whole class marking, peer or self-marking in class, use of short multiple-choice quizzes and questioning techniques as checks in class.[218]

- School leaders and teachers need to work together to change the culture of long working hours in their school. For teachers, Ben Newmark has written a compelling blog suggesting teachers try to make unreasonable demands visible by working at school, rather than at home.[219] As a school leader, if you spot a teacher frequently working long hours, take responsibility for the workload problem they clearly face and work collaboratively to fix it.

- Think about which weeks in your school year are particularly draining. For example, what parts of the process of report writing and parent's evenings are essential to keep pupil learning on track? How do you *know* they are essential? Many schools are experimenting with new ways of communicating with parents that are less burdensome for both sides and more connected to the child's learning.[220]

CHAPTER EIGHT

Teaching teachers
What policymakers can do without waiting for schools

Responsibility for initial teacher training in England has swung back and forth between schools and training colleges over the decades. A cynic might comment that we keep one model only as long as it takes us to forget the drawbacks of the other. At present, we have a pluralistic system which involves several different version of each model. At one extreme is Teach First, which runs basic 'crash courses' on the theory of teaching in a summer school, after which novices are left to sink-or-swim, teaching a slightly reduced timetable in schools which have teacher shortages. At the other extreme is the long-established university-based post-graduate certificate, which involves a nine-month period of university instruction twinned with two, loosely integrated, school placements. All ITT programmes involve some element of learning on the job and academic input.[221] However, all of the training models are hopelessly front-loaded and the integration between the academic and practice elements of the training routes is often non-existent. In our view, little or none of the existing provision gives teachers the opportunity to practice evidence-based techniques in realistic environments with the help of an expert coach giving them sufficient feedback. We believe that this is an important part of the explanation for the relentless decline in early-career retention and the stagnation of standards observed by

Professor Coe. In this chapter, we set out a diagnosis of what is wrong with initial teacher training and a prescription for how to solve it.

Gary Becker, the Nobel prize-winning economist from Chicago, popularised the term "human capital" to describe the personal stock of knowledge, skills, habits and other attributes that make us productive in the workplace. Human, because they reside within each person. Capital, because these are resources which can be developed through investment and then reused time and again. Economic theory suggests that human capital tends to benefit employers by making their employees more productive, and benefits workers by enhancing the wage they can command in the workplace. Teachers' human capital also benefits pupils, by accelerating their learning. But Becker noticed that, despite increased human capital seeming to be good for everyone, individuals and the firms who employ them often neglect to invest in it.[222]

Two of his insights in particular shed light on why the current market for initial teacher training is not delivering the skills teachers need to sustain a productive career in the classroom. First, the skills we need novice teachers to acquire are quite general skills in the sense that, once learnt, they will be useful working in any school. Second, the market for schools who need to employ teachers is characterised by over 20,000 small institutions, independently hiring and training staff. These two facts combine to produce a market that, Becker observed, would lead individual schools to underinvest in teacher training. After all, if an individual school trains a teacher, then there is no guarantee that they can recoup the considerable time investment of supporting a novice teacher. The teachers might well just move on to another school and use their skills there instead. Equally, other schools are small enough to adopt a 'free-rider' strategy, leaving the training of teachers to other, more selfless schools, and scooping up trained teachers in the labour market, as and when they need them.[223]

Becker said that, since firms would not pay for general training in these circumstances, individuals would have to pay instead, perhaps through accepting a lower wage in return for the training. This would make schools more relaxed about not recouping their investment, since they would already have benefited from the cheap labour. However, as two more economists, Acemoglu and Pischke later pointed out, this does not solve the problem entirely. Individual trainees often wouldn't be able to force a decent quality of training to take place once they had been recruited to a school. This is known as a 'hold-up' problem: once you have taken the training job, you are stuck there for the year, and so the school can short-change you on their promise of training, safe in the knowledge that they will still get access to your cheap labour.[224] No doubt, many enlightened, ethical schools would still offer high quality training for the good of the profession. The problem is that inevitably some would not, and trainees would find it hard to distinguish the good from the bad. Acquiring nuanced information on twenty thousand schools is a tricky task! Like Ellen, many newly qualified teachers may not even know what they are looking for. All of this means the market for teacher training is likely delivering far less human capital than employers, employees and pupils would like it to be.

Since the mid-twentieth century, universities have been the main procurers of training placements for teachers in England. They too find it quite hard to ascertain which schools and departments will offer a good training experience. Working with a school over a number of years will of course provide them with a sense of whether they are capable of supporting a trainee. But the departure of one or two key staff from the school can change this overnight. Moreover, because the cash payments offered to schools for hosting trainees are small, universities have minimal bargaining power to make schools up their game, or to tempt in new schools which may (or may not) be better equipped to support trainees.

Ironically, the main thing propping up the market for initial teacher training at the moment is the severe shortage of teachers. Many schools are willing to take on trainees on the basis that they will have first refusal on them once qualified. However, this use of training placements as a recruitment device has a couple of quirks. One is that long lead times on recruitment mean that schools cannot efficiently hire trainees to match their needs. Secondary schools need many different types of specialist subject teachers, meaning that their demand for teachers is simply too unpredictable. Training science and maths teachers will always be a safe bet, since schools need lots of them and there is a severe shortage. But for smaller shortage subjects such as music or religious studies, the incentives to take on trainees is weak.

Even worse, because it is the low performing and disadvantaged schools that suffer from staffing shortages, the schools with the strongest incentives to take on trainees are often not those that are best placed to support them. High performing schools with excellent working conditions generally have less need to recruit new teachers. As a result, those schools with the greatest strength and stability to deliver training experiences are often not the institutions who are incentivised to do so. It's the same adverse selection that Ellen experienced. To fix this, we need to solve both problems highlighted by the economists: the weak incentives for good schools to take on trainees and the lack of information about which schools offer good training. This will in turn require two big reforms. The first is an institution, or set of institutions, that are able to collect accurate information on which schools have the capability to provide high quality training placements. The second is a system of payments that make it worthwhile for reluctant schools to train novice teachers.

The teachers we have met so far in this book have all been real. The last teacher we will introduce, Mia, is not. Instead of illustrating something that the research tells us about the current state of the profession, she instead serves to illustrate how an evidence-based reform of the profession could transform the early career experience. There are no carefully-controlled studies evaluating the wide-ranging reform we set out below. There probably never could be. With Mia's story we are instead drawing on all the ideas and empirical evidence we have discussed in the book up to this point: the job demand-resources model; adverse selection; learning curves; the limits to learning from experience; working memory; habits; self-determination theory; the free rider problem. There are plenty of specifics in what follows, but the thrust of the argument is more important than the details. If you can see how these conclusions follow logically from what we have set out in the previous six chapters, then we will have achieved our aim.

*　*　*

Mia finished her maths degree in 2021. She had been so busy studying for exams every summer since 2018 that she hadn't given much thought to what she would do after graduation. She was certainly in demand, but Mia couldn't quite picture herself working for a bank or the civil service. Her older sister Nicky had graduated four years earlier and then become a teacher. Although Mia had never seriously considered teaching herself, she was always rapt listening to her sister's warts and all accounts of life in the classroom. There was something about it which appealed.

That June, partly out of curiosity, Mia registered her interest in teaching on a government website. An email immediately came back, setting out what she could expect from her local initial teacher-training programme. It explained that, each year, schools bid to take on trainee teachers. The right to host a trainee teacher is then allocated to schools by the regional teacher training institution, based on the support that schools offer to provide and their track record in retaining staff, including trainees. The bids are assessed on a number of criteria relating to the demands of the role they are offering and the support provided by the school. Secondary schools generally guarantee their trainees that they will only have to teach one subject, usually the one in which they have a degree, for the duration of the year. They also compete by offering trainees access to lesson plans prepared by their experienced teachers and providing dedicated coaches who teach the same subject or year group. The email informed her that, if she was accepted, she would be allocated to one of the successful schools in September to teach a one-third timetable. After spending a year there, she would then be allocated to another nearby school for the second year, on a two-thirds timetable. At the end of her two one-year placements she would receive her teaching diploma and could then apply for a job in any school she liked.

Mia felt reassured that schools were brandishing their credentials in supporting trainees and relieved that somebody else had done the hard work of filtering out the lemons. The pledges to limit her assignments and provide a coach also helped ease her fears about whether she was up to the job.

In August, Mia attended a gruelling summer school with her cohort of trainees. The initial summer school taught her the basic routines of teaching, such as how to get pupils into and out of a class-room in an orderly way, how to command attention in a room, and how to adapt lesson plans. The course was jointly provided by school staff and a nearby university, whose expertise was bought in by the host school. However, the distinction here was pretty blurred, since school-based trainers and academic researchers often moved back and forth between roles. At no stage, however, would Mia be enrolled on a lengthy programme of full-time university study, as teachers were in the past. There was some reading involved, but not a great deal in the first year. The emphasis was instead placed on practising specific techniques with immediate feedback from the coaches. Mia found practising the techniques a little artificial and awkward at first, but soon came to see the value in it.

At the beginning of September, she began teaching an hour or two of maths each day at St Michael's Secondary School. Her teaching coach, Anne, who had trained at St Michael's four years earlier, was a constant, reassuring presence. They would have lunch together most days and Anne would often check in with her at the end of the day for a quick debrief. Mia was glad to have somebody that she could ask the 'stupid' questions to. Anne and the rest of the teachers in the maths department shared their lesson plans and resources. This freed up Mia to focus on the already overwhelming task of keeping order and explaining the material with clarity. The Head of Department was also careful to keep demands for paperwork under control, encouraging all staff to use an online homework system to provide feedback on how all pupils in the school were progressing each week. Beyond her maths teaching, the school did not expect her to supervise a form class, break times or detentions. Instead, they gently encouraged her to restrict her extra-curricular involvements in that first year. That didn't stop Mia falling asleep on her sofa at 10pm every evening that first term, exhausted.

All of the teachers in the maths department took the responsibility of training Mia seriously. They knew their ability to host trainees in the future depended partly on whether Mia went on to a sustained career in teaching. St Michaels wanted to provide training place-ments because it provided them with privileged information about the quality of new trainees. It also helped them retain talented mid-career teachers who themselves wanted to train as coaches – a career route that had come to be seen as equally prestigious, and far more interesting, than school management. This in turn benefited the host schools, who used the coaches and the engagement with nearby universities to support the development of all their staff. Perhaps more important than any of this, however, was the amount of money attached to each trainee. The fees paid to schools by the local teacher training institution were adjusted to ensure that a sufficient number of high quality training places were available in each region and for each subject and phase. If not enough high quality placements are offered by schools in a specific subject or phase then the fees were increased. If there was a surplus then they were frozen. This meant it was always worthwhile for schools like St Michaels to host trainees.

During term time, Mia spent one day a week on her formal training. The sessions combined seminars led by academic researchers with practise of evidence-based techniques guided by expert coaches. The trainers knew how demanding the first two years in the classroom are and recognised that their trainee's bandwidth was a scarce resource. They also worked with teachers in years three, four and five of their training and knew that the more advanced content could be assimilated much more effectively by teachers later in their career. So they focused instead on helping Mia and her colleagues become fluent in the basics. Mia gradually found her knowledge and skills growing as a result. She looked forward to these sessions just as much as a chance to catch up with trainees from other schools and exchange notes on difficult pupils and disastrous lessons. When the seminar leaders left at the end of the session, Mia and the other trainees would invariably head to the pub to continue the conversation over a drink.

By the summer term, Mia could feel she was in greater control in the classroom. Nine months of learning through trial and error had given her a strong sense of what didn't work. She was careful to avoid overcomplicating her lessons. She knew which types of questions didn't get a response. She was quicker to adapt her approach when the students didn't respond well to an explanation – somehow she had more capacity to recalculate and change course mid-flight.

Mia felt pride in the progress she was making and this sense of success was reinforced by the feedback she received. When the summer holidays arrived she was tired, but more enthusiastic than ever about teaching.

At Mia's second August summer school she noticed a step up in the sophistication of the material they were being taught by the seminar leaders. She had read about feedback methods during her first year, but that summer was the first time she really thought about her approach. Indeed, they talked about little else for those four weeks. Guided by their coach, the group discussed the evidence base and practised specific techniques. The seminar leaders were consistent in prompting trainees to consider what doesn't add value. They warned her how difficult it would be to incorporate these new techniques into her existing classroom practice, but through repeated and deliberate practice Mia was slowly able to adapt how she taught.

Mia's new school, Oaktree Academy, was in many ways similar to St Michael's. Her new mentor was not as responsive as Anne was, but her colleagues were friendly and more open to discussing teaching practice. Mia was pleasantly surprised to see staff generally left the school by 4pm each day, not least because management had centralised burdens such as behaviour management systems and had minimal data demands in place. When Mia reflected on these differences in the staffroom, a more experienced colleague gave her the back-story. Three years ago, the staff at the school had become demoralised by management practices and voted with their feet. The school's retention figures became so poor that other teachers were discouraged from applying for jobs there and they were barred from taking on trainees to fill the gaps. Eventually the school leadership had been forced to act, bringing workload under control, stemming the loss of teachers and eventually regaining the right to host trainees. It all prompted Mia to think carefully about the type of department she wanted to work in. She made a mental note of the specific questions she would ask when she interviewed for post-certification jobs at the end of the year. Her colleagues in the maths department were all keen to offer advice on what to look for. They also knew their ability to host trainees in future would be influenced by whether Mia continued in the profession.

Not all of Mia's peer group were having such a positive experience. When she began her training there were twenty in her seminar group, but only eighteen made it to the end of the second year. One of the trainees that hadn't made it, Ben, had decided that teaching just wasn't for him. His school had tried everything to persuade him to stay but he had handed in his notice at the end of his first year. In his exit interview, routinely conducted by the local teacher training institution with all trainees who leave within the first four years, Ben confirmed that the school had provided him with a manageable teaching assignment and good mentoring. The school's overall retention figures remained good and, as a result, they maintained their contract for hosting trainees in the following year.

The other dropout, Alice, had a very different experience. Her mentor had been distant and inaccessible and, while the other teachers in the department were nice to her, they were busy with their own work. She found the coaching useful, but her pupils were more difficult than Mia's, in part because the overall behaviour policy at Alice's school was weaker. This made it harder to deploy what she had learned. It also left her feeling like she wasn't doing a good job. She began staying later in the evenings and working all day on Sundays to try and bullet-proof her resources and lesson plans. She struggled to find time for friends and family. Half way through the Easter term, her Head of Department noticed that Alice's pupils were progressing slowly and began observing her lessons and providing detailed advice. Alice hated the observations but was determined to learn from them, working even harder to show she was taking all the comments on board. She felt she was making some progress, but by now she was in a fog of workload, unable to recognise her own achievements. By the summer term she began to feel resentment towards the other teachers in her department and, even when she got a good night's sleep, she would wake up without the energy for the day ahead. In her exit interview with the local teacher training provider, she was apologetic and even embarrassed to be quitting, but she knew she couldn't continue. She described her experience at the school in detail and the local teacher training institution put all the information on file, and began a review of her school's capacity to host trainees the following year.

Fortunately, Mia had a better placement, and by the final term of the training programme, she felt secure in her own abilities as a teacher. But there was also something lacking. In her first year, she had been able to look back on a term and see clearly how she had improved over the twelve weeks. She could point to specific instances where she had messed something up, learnt her lesson, and become a better teacher as a result. But by her sixth term, getting things wrong had become a matter of degree. She still got the warm glow from working with trusted colleagues and delivering a great lesson, but she was yearning for that feeling of growth which she had been become accustomed to. She had learned by now that improving her teaching could only be achieved through the hard graft of practice, but also that finding the right colleagues and coaches could help accelerate the process. She had been offered a job at St Michael's but she wanted to be sure there was nothing better on offer. So she sat down once again with her sister Nicky, who had just become a fully-qualified teacher after six years in the classroom, to choose her next school. After all, with the skills and experience she had already acquired, schools would be lucky to have her.

*   *   *

Mia's story illustrates how we can solve the problems identified by economists. First, by providing payments to schools for year-long training placements, schools are incentivised to provide careful training for teachers, even if they cannot guarantee that the trainees will stay working with them. The level of these payments needs to be flexible and dynamic in order to ensure that the market for high quality training places clears each year – that is the number of high quality training places offered by schools equals the number required by government. Second, by organising the procurement of placements in permanent, regional, teacher training institutions, it becomes possible to collect information on the quality of training placements offered by schools and ensure that teachers are given the support they need, rather than being short changed. It is critically important that both of these reforms are introduced simultaneously.

The incentives are necessary to improve quality and the information is necessary to provide the incentives.

We have also used Mia's story to illustrate how such a reform could be used to abolish the front-loaded model of initial teacher training and replace it with a longer, thinner approach to take account of the slow, sequential way in which all people, including teachers, develop skills. In Mia's case, we described a two-year period of training before teachers receive their teaching diploma, followed by a further four years before teachers receive fully qualified status. We propose teachers should be given one-third of a standard teaching timetable in year one (e.g. around 8 hours a week) and two-thirds of a standard teaching timetable in year two, in order to reduce the demands placed on trainees. The longer initial teacher-training period would allow trainers to sequence new content and techniques over a longer period, allowing more practice and feedback before moving on to new material. Both the diploma and the full qualification should have a strong emphasis on coaching and deliberate practice to ensure that what is taught is integrated securely into teachers' classroom practice. Both qualifications should be mandatory.

This long training route would be comparable with the way medicine is organised in England: doctors become "registered" one year after medical school and then graduate from their status as Junior Doctors around five years after that. It would also bring us into line with our European neighbours, where the minimum total duration of teacher training is often between four and six years. The length of the training period between receiving the diploma and achieving fully qualified status could also be left variable, as it is for doctors, to reflect the other commitments of teachers (whether personal or professional) and to accommodate specialist training routes, such as special education.

As well as paying for the training placements during the diploma period, government should also fund the training leading to fully qualified teacher status. The alternative – requiring schools to fund it from their existing budgets – would skew the incentives for employing teachers during this period of their career. It would also hold down wages, which would likely reduce retention further, given how sensitive teachers are to pay during the early years of their career.[225] Funding for the second stage of the qualification should therefore follow the teachers and be routed through schools. In some ways, this is similar to the government's new apprenticeship model.[226] We believe the subsidies, regulation and extension of the qualification period are essential components of making such a reform effective. It is likely that government will also need to subsidise the coaching qualifications for experienced teachers until their status, and thus value to schools and teachers, is established. These can be purchased 'off the shelf' using models which have been shown to be effective in replicated randomised controlled trials.[227]

There are two important potential objections to our proposal. The first objection is that the reduced timetable and tripling of the length of training will cause a large increase in the cost of training new teachers. We agree that costs would increase, but there are a number of reasons that this increase will not be substantial. First, our model would give trainees a similar or even larger class allocation than the existing university-led PGCE model, which is effectively zero in year one (because all classes belong to another teacher who remains employed by the school) and 90 per cent of a full timetable in year two. Giving trainees ownership of classes, albeit only for a fraction of the timetable covered by a fully qualified teacher, ensures that they have productive value to schools, just as trainee doctors and nurses do to hospitals. This will help hold down the value of the incentive that the government will have to offer when purchasing these training placements.[228] Second, if our proposal works, it will increase early career retention. The current cost per trainee is in fact a gross underestimate of the cost of generating an experienced teacher, since a third of trainees leave within four years. The real cost per expert teacher created is therefore a multiple of the cost per trainee.[229] Increasing retention though improved ITT reduces this multiplier, reducing the cost of training each additional, experienced teacher.

A second objection to our proposal is that it will harm some struggling schools because they will no longer be able to recruit teachers through training placements. Again, we agree with this analysis. In the short run, our reforms would cause severe staffing problems for a small number of schools that are currently relying on a recruit–burnout–replace staffing model. These schools may need additional support during this period.[230] However, stripped of the ability to recruit naïve trainees, they would soon be forced to improve working conditions in order to improve retention. In the long run, we argue that our proposal would help eliminate teacher shortages, ensuring that there are enough well-trained teachers for all schools to be well staffed. We therefore see this as a virtue of our proposals, rather than a drawback. It certainly would have helped Ella.

CHAPTER NINE

A career worth having

In the introduction, we looked at Professor Rob Coe's bleak assessment of English education over the past twenty years: "Standards have not risen; teaching has not improved." We posed the question: how it could be that twenty years of near-constant reform, and at times lavish spending, has achieved so little? By now, the answer should be clear. A cocktail of policy changes and school leadership practices, generally introduced with the best of intentions, have conspired to undermine the teaching profession, creating an expanding gap between the quantity and quality of teachers we need, and the quantity and quality of teachers that we have.

In Chapter 2, we saw the decisive influence of teacher quality on pupil progress and the powerful performance-enhancing effects of learning from experience. In Chapter 3, however, we saw how teachers like Abi and James get ejected from the profession before they have a chance to learn the ropes. The predictable result was that two potentially great teachers left the profession and were replaced by two more novices. What else would we expect when the demands placed on them were so disproportionate to the support available? This merry go-round has dizzyingly destructive effects on the overall quality of teaching in our schools. In Chapter 4, we saw how apparently good schools get away with running sausage-machine recruitment models in which teachers are hired, burned out and replaced, year after year. The result is that even teachers like Ellen, who would love to be back in the classroom, can't bring themselves to apply for another teaching job, too wary of picking another lemon. Ellen was either replaced by yet another newly-qualified teacher or, more likely, not replaced at all. And so the teacher gap grows wider still. In Chapter 5 we saw how even those teachers like Luke, who survive the first few years on the job and acquire valuable skills, find themselves being pushed out. Incentive schemes designed to motivate teachers are in fact undermining their love of their job and increasing the size of the gap. Then, in Chapter 6, we saw how most professional development is hopelessly ineffective, leaving old habits in place and bringing teachers' ascent up the learning curve to a standstill. The result is that teachers become demotivated, even bored, and fail to realise their potential in the classroom. In Chapter 7, we saw how the gap between the reality of good teaching and the paper trail required to audit classroom activities only serves to undermine teachers' motivation further still. Over the years, these policies and practices have widened the gap to a chasm. It is all our own doing.

Closing the gap requires us to make teaching a career worth having. We have argued at length that this can only be achieved by treating teachers as autonomous professionals and recognising that they are naturally inclined to develop and improve if given the right challenge and support. By making the job more attractive we can create a prestigious profession with competitive entry and sufficient supply so that headteachers can employ teachers in whom they have confidence.

Getting to this destination will, however, be difficult, because we are starting from a point of fragility and dysfunction. Shortages mean that many teachers are given too much responsibility too early. It's not uncommon for teachers to find themselves managing an entire department three years into their career. We think it should take them twice that long just to qualify! The same shortages mean headteachers are often unable to recruit the kind of staff they would ideally want to teach in their schools. Unsettled by this, and the blunt-force pressure exerted on them by the accountability system, they double down on audit, generating ever more requests for the

generation of 'evidence' that learning is taking place. The inspectorate, many of whom were heads in a bygone era, help fossilise these
defensive management practices by demanding to see this audit trail.
Meanwhile the government is strapped for cash and unable to recruit
the number of teachers it needs to compensate for increased attrition
from the profession. Workload posters won't be sufficient to untangle
this knot.

So what will?

We believe that it is within the gift of school leaders to substantially change how they manage their teachers, without waiting
for policymakers to make any changes and we have given examples
of how this could be done throughout the book. The first steps will
be risky – leaders are, after all, under intense pressure to get results.
But we don't for a minute think that school leaders enjoy doing the
job the way they do now. They must instead relearn the art of trust,
get back in the habit of defending work–life balance and refocus their
energies away from management-by-numbers onto supporting the
professional growth of their staff.

Of course, not all teachers can and will thrive in a trust culture.
Those that cannot must therefore be managed out in order to
maintain the viability of the profession for the benefit of teachers
and pupils. Audit systems should be restricted for use on this tiny
minority of teachers who are unsuited to the job. Headteachers
and teaching unions should work together in the interests of the
wider profession to ensure that teachers in this position are treated
as humanely as possible, with support to find alternative careers.
As headteacher Stephen Tierney describes it: "you deal with the
exceptions; what you don't do is build a universal system around it
that affects all teachers and school leaders."[231]

Policymakers must enable leaders to work in autonomy-supportive
ways without risking their own career. Anecdotally, Ofsted appears
to be reducing the extent to which it demands excessive paper trails
during school inspections. But it is too early to tell whether this
represents a consistent, sustained change in behaviour. The danger
is that, with only a single day to inspect schools, the inspectorate
falls back into old habits of demanding 'evidence' for things which
cannot or should not be measured. If there is any risk that not having

the necessary paperwork in place will endanger a headteacher's job, they will continue to audit. Inspectors therefore need to make a credible commitment to school leaders. If short inspections are not sufficient to judge the quality of a school without Ofsted requiring elaborate audit trails, then short inspections should be abolished. Teachers spending the majority of their week on activities only tangentially related to pupil learning is not a price worth paying to sustain the inspectorate in its current form.

Policymakers must also make it impossible for dysfunctional schools to operate recruit–burnout–replace staffing models without consequences. This damages the pipeline of talent for all schools and puts the entire profession under greater strain. Funnel plots provide a simple, fair and inexpensive way of identifying which schools are misusing new teachers in this way. Too often, league tables and accountability metrics have been used as a tool for piling more pressure onto the teaching profession. Putting information about turnover levels in the hands of regulators or teachers would instead empower them. School leaders are often quick to transmit account-ability pressure down on to their staff. In the long run this is of course counterproductive, driving teachers out of the profession. But faced with the clear and present danger of losing their job from a bad inspection result, this is a trade-off some are willing to take. Using funnel plots to help teachers avoid these schools would force school leaders to internalise these trade-offs by making sausage machines unsustainable.

Finally, it is in the area of initial teacher training where we believe government intervention and reform is most needed. In other comparable professions, the length of the qualification covers the entire period where sustained training is needed. This is why we believe teachers in England should work towards a teaching diploma on a form of apprenticeship contract over two years, receiving structured coaching on a reduced timetable. They should then work through more advanced and specialist courses, as doctors do, over the next two to four years to achieve their masters or fully- qualified teacher status. Policymakers need to set up the institutions capable of assessing the quality of training placements and stump up the cash to incentivise good schools to offer them. Incorporating school turnover information into the bidding process for hosting trainees would reinforce the message and incentives that schools need to look after their staff.

Educational standards in England have not risen, but it could be so much different if we focus on the point of greatest leverage: teachers. The good news for school leaders is that there is a great deal they can do without waiting for policymakers. The good news for policymakers is that there are many things they can do to help. For the sake of pupils, the two must work together to ensure that that teaching is once again a career worth having.

Notes and references

1   Lance, L. (2011). Non-production benefits of education: crime, health, and good citizenship. In E.A. Hanushek, S. Machin and L. Woessman (eds), *Handbook of the economics of education* (pp. 183–282). Amsterdam, the Netherlands: Elsevier.

2   Grade inflation is the phenomenon whereby increasing numbers of pupils are awarded the higher grades or marks each year, without demonstrating correspondingly higher levels of subject competency in tests.

3   Coe, R. and Tymms, P. (2008). Summary of research on changes in educational standards in the UK. In M. Harris (ed.), *Education briefing book 2008: IoD policy paper*. London: Institute of Directors.

Shayer, M., Ginsburg, D., and Coe, R. (2007). Thirty Years on – a large anti-Flynn effect? The Piagetian test Volume and Heaviness norms 1975–2003. *British Journal of Educational Psychology*, 77(1), 25–41.

Tymms, P., and Merrell, C. (2007). *Standards and quality in English primary schools over time: The national evidence* (Primary Review Research Survey 4/1), Cambridge, UK: University of Cambridge Faculty of Education.

Hodgen, J., Kuchemann, D., Brown, M., and Coe, R. (2009). Children's understandings of algebra 30 years on. *Research in Mathematics Education*, 11(2), 193–194.

Hodgen, J., Küchemann, D., Brown, M., and Coe, R. (2010). Multiplicative reasoning, ratio and decimals: A 30-year comparison of lower secondary students' understandings. In M. F. Pinto and T. F. Kawaski (eds.), *Proceedings of the 34th conference of the international group of the psychology of mathematics education* (Vol. 3, pp. 89–96). Brazil: Belo Horizonte.

4   Rashid, S., and Brooks, G. (2010). *The levels of attainment in literacy and numeracy of 13- to 19-year-olds in England, 1948–2009*. London: NRDC.

5   Blanden, J., Gregg, P., and Macmillan, L. (2007). Accounting for intergenerational income persistence: Non-cognitive skills, ability and education. *The Economic Journal*, 117, C43–C60.

6   Lupton, R., Thomson, S., and Obolenskaya, P. (2016). Schools. In R. Lupton, T. Burchardt, J. Hills, K. Stewart, and P. Vizard (eds), *Social policy in a cold climate: Policies and their consequences since the crisis* (pp. 59–80). Bristol, UK: Policy Press.

7   Thomson, D. (2016). *The short run impact of the Building Schools for the Future programme on attainment at key stage 4*, Department of Social Science Working Paper No. 16–07, UCL Institute of Education.

8   *ibid.*

9   Allen, R., and Burgess, S. (2010). *The future of competition and accountability in education*, 2020 Public Services Trust at the RSA report.

10   Angrist, J.D., Lavy, V., Leder-Luis, J., and Shany, A. (2017). *Maimonides rule redux*, National Bureau of Economic Research working paper w23486.

Average annual progress for a Grade 6 (Year 7) pupil in the US, see: Hill, C.J., Bloom, H.S., and Lipsey, M.W. (2007). *Empirical benchmarks for interpreting effect sizes in research acknowledgments*, MDRC working papers on research methodology (July). Retrieved from: www.mdrc.org/sites/default/files/full_84.pdf.

11   Holmlund, H., McNally, S., and Viarengo, M. (2009). *Does money matter for schools?* CEE discussion paper 105, London School of Economics.

12   Croft, J. (2015). *Why collaboration probably isn't key to the next phase of school reform*, CMRE Research report 7, Centre for the Study of Market Reform of Education.

13   Van Reenen, J. (2012, May 28). *It is time to move away from policy witchcraft and into an era where evidence is taken seriously*

[Blog post]. Retrieved from: http://blogs.lse.ac.uk/politicsandpolicy/evidence-based-policy-beecroft-van-reenen/.

14   Slater, H., Davies, N., and Burgess, S. (2012). Do teachers matter? Measuring the variation in teacher effectiveness in England. *Oxford Bulletin of Economics and Statistics*, 74, 629–645.

Hanushek, E.A., and Rivkin, S.G. (2012). The distribution of teacher quality and implications for policy. *Annual Review of Economics*, 4, 131–157.

15   Wiliam, D. (2016). *Leadership for teacher learning: Creating a culture where all teachers improve so that all students succeed*. West Palm Beach, FL: Learning Sciences International.

16   Hamre, B.K., and Pianta, R.C. (2005). Can instructional and emotional support in the first-grade classroom make a difference for children at risk of school failure? *Child Development*, 76(5), 949–967.

Slater, H., Davies, N., and Burgess, S. (2012). Do teachers matter? Measuring the variation in teacher effectiveness in England. *Oxford Bulletin of Economics and Statistics*, 74, 629–645.

17   Chetty, R., Friedman, J.N., and Rockoff, J.E. (2014). Measuring the impacts of teachers II: Teacher value-added and student outcomes in adulthood. *American Economic Review*, 104(9), 2633–2679.

18   Griva, K., and Joekes, K. (2003). UK teachers under stress: Can we predict wellness on the basis of characteristics of the teaching job? *Psychology and Health*, 18(4), 457–471.

19   Cooper, J.M., and Alvarado, A. (2006). *Preparation, recruitment, and retention of teachers*. Paris: International Institute for Educational Planning.

20   The £700m includes costs to central government (including bursaries, grants to schools, tuition costs, maintenance loans and grants) and costs to schools (including the cost of staff time and other fees). See: National Audit Office (2016). *Training new teachers*, NAO report HC 798 Session 2015–16. Retrieved from: www.nao.org.uk/wp-content/uploads/2016/02/Training-new-teachers.pdf.

21   Syed, M. (2015). *Black box thinking*. London: John Murray.

22   Kraft, M.A., and Papay, J.P. (2014). Can professional environments in schools promote teacher development? Explaining heterogeneity in returns to teaching experience. *Educational Evaluation and Policy Analysis*, 36(4), 476–500.

This is not driven by differential sample attrition: Papay, J.P., and Kraft, M.A. (2015). Productivity returns to experience in the teacher labor market: Methodological challenges and new evidence on long-term career improvement. *Journal of Public Economics, 130,* 105–119.

23   Minstrell, J. (1999). Expertise in teaching. In R. Sternberg and J.A. Horvath (eds), *Tacit knowledge in professional practice: Researcher and practitioner perspectives.* Mahwah, NJ: Lawrence Erlbaum.

24   Patel, V.L., Arocha, J.F., and Kaufman, D.R. (1999). Expertise and tacit knowledge in medicine. In R. Sternberg and J.A Horvath (eds), *Tacit knowledge in professional practice: Researcher and practitioner perspectives.* Mahwah, NJ: Lawrence Erlbaum.

25   Brown University (2015). *UEP Professors Matthew A. Kraft and John P. Papay win the 2015 AERA Palmer O. Johnson Award!* [Brown University Urban Education Policy Blog]. Retrieved from: https://brownuepblog.wordpress.com/2015/03/31/aera.

26   Kraft, M.A., and Papay, J.P. (2014). Can professional environments in schools promote teacher development? Explaining heterogeneity in returns to teaching experience. *Educational Evaluation and Policy Analysis,* 36(4), 476–500.

27   Ost, B., and Schiman, J.C. (2015). Grade-specific experience, grade reassignments, and teacher turnover. *Economics of Education Review,* 46, 112–126.

28   Goldhaber, D., Krieg, J.M., and Theobald, R. (2017). Does the match matter? Exploring whether student teaching experiences affect teacher effectiveness. *American Educational Research Journal,* 54(2), 325–359.

29   Atteberry, A., Loeb, S., and Wyckoff, J. (2016). Teacher churning reassignment rates and implications for student achievement. *Educational Evaluation and Policy Analysis,* 39(1), 3–30.

30   Penuel, W.R., Sun, M., Frank, K.A., and Gallagher, H.A. (2012). Using social network analysis to study how collegial interactions can augment teacher learning from external professional development. *American Journal of Education,* 119(1), 103–136.

Sun, M., Penuel, W.R., Frank, K.A., Gallagher, H.A., and Youngs, P. (2013). Shaping professional development to promote the diffusion of instructional expertise among teachers. *Educational Evaluation and Policy Analysis,* 35(3), 344–369.

31   Loeb, S., Kalogrides, D., and Béteille, T. (2012). Effective schools: Teacher hiring, assignment, development, and retention. *Education Finance and Policy,* 7, 269–304.

Jackson, C.K., and Bruegmann, E. (2009). Teaching students and teaching each other: The importance of peer learning for teachers. *American Economic Journal: Applied Economics*, 1(4), 85–108.

32   *ibid.*

33   See Online Appendix A in Kraft, M.A., and Papay, J.P. (2014). Can professional environments in schools promote teacher development? Explaining heterogeneity in returns to teaching experience. *Educational Evaluation and Policy Analysis*, 36(4), 476–500.

34   Polanyi, M. (1966). *The tacit dimension*, Chicago, IL: University of Chicago Press.

35   For a discussion of ostensive tacit knowledge (knowledge that can be pointed to, but not explicated) and the role of socialisation in transferring it, see pages 93–100 of Collins, H. (2010). *Tacit and explicit knowledge*. Chicago, IL: University of Chicago Press.

36   Supovitz, J., Sirinides, P., and May, H. (2009). How principals and peers influence teaching and learning. *Educational Administration Quarterly*, 46(1), 31–56.

Hallinger, P., and Heck, R.H. (1998). Exploring the principal's contribution to school effectiveness: 1980–1995. *School Effectiveness and School Improvement*, 9(2), 157–191.

37   Papay, J.P., Taylor, E.S., Tyler, J.H., and Laski, M. (2016). *Learning job skills from colleagues at work: Evidence from a field experiment using teacher performance data* (No. w21986). National Bureau of Economic Research.

38   That medics spend six years at university before starting full time work doesn't change the fact that training is delivered in this sequential pattern.

39   See page 9 in Allen, R., Belfield, C., Greaves, E., Sharp, C., and Walker, M. (2014). *The costs and benefits of different initial teacher training routes*, IFS Report R100, Institute for Fiscal Studies.

40   Ericsson, K.A. (2004). Deliberate practice and the acquisition and maintenance of expert performance in medicine and related domains. *Academic Medicine: Journal of the Association of American Medical Colleges*, 79, S70–S81.

Hambrick, D.Z., Oswald, F.L., Altmann, E.M., Meinz, E.J., Gobet, F., and Campitelli, G. (2014). Deliberate practice: Is that all it takes to become an expert? *Intelligence*, 45, 34–45.

41   Berliner, D. C. (1994). A model of teaching expertise. In National Evaluation Systems (ed.), *Continuing discussions in teacher certification*

testing. Retrieved from: http://images.pearsonassessments.com/ images/NES_Publications/1994_05Berliner_339_1.pdf.

42   Feldon, D.F. (2007). Cognitive load and classroom teaching: The double-edged sword of automaticity. *Educational Psychologist*, 42(3), 123–137.

43   van Merriënboer, J. (2016). How people learn. In N. Rushby and D.W. Surry (eds), *The Wiley handbook of learning technology*. Hoboken, NJ: John Wiley and Sons.

44   Carter, K., Cushing, K., Sabers, D., Stein, P., and Berliner, D.C. (1988). Expert-novice differences in perceiving and processing visual information. *Journal of Teacher Education*, 39(3), 25–31.

      Lin, S.S.J. (1999). *Looking for the prototype of teaching expertise: An initial attempt in Taiwan*. Paper presented at the meetings of the American Educational Research Association, Boston, MA.

      Sato, M., Akita, K., and Iwakawa, N. (1993). Practical thinking styles of teachers: A comparative study of expert and novice thought processes and its implications for rethinking teacher education in Japan. *Peabody Journal of Education*, 68, 100–110.

45   Moos, D.C., and Pitton, D. (2014). Student teacher challenges: Using the cognitive load theory as an explanatory lens. *Teaching Education*, 25(2), 127–141.

46   Sims, S., Moss, G., and Marshall, M. (2017). Teacher journal clubs: How do they work and can they increase evidence-based practice? *Impact: The Journal of the Royal College of Teaching*, 1(1).

47   Kane, M.T. (2017). Measurement error and bias in value-added models. *ETS Research Report Series*. doi:10.1002/ets2.12153.

48   Slater, H., Davies, N.M., and Burgess, S. (2012). Do teachers matter? Measuring the variation in teacher effectiveness in England. *Oxford Bulletin of Economics and Statistics*, 74(5), 629–645.

49   McCaffrey, D.F., Sass, T.R., Lockwood, J.R., and Mihaly, K. (2009). The intertemporal variability of teacher effect estimates. *Education Finance and Policy*, 4(4), 572–606.

50   Kane, T.J., McCaffrey, D.F., Miller, T., and Staiger, O. (2013). *Have we identified effective teachers? Validating measures of effective teaching Using Random Assignment*. MET Project Research Paper: Bill and Melinda Gates Foundation.

51   Chetty, R., Friedman, J.N., and Rockoff, J.E. (2014). Measuring the impacts of teachers II: Teacher value-added and outcomes in adulthood. *American Economic Review*, 104(9), 2633–2679.

52   Research suggests that teachers from different departments can help each other improve: Papay, J.P., Taylor, E.S., Tyler, J.H., and Laski, M. (2016). *Learning job skills from colleagues at work: Evidence from a field experiment using teacher performance data* (No. w21986). National Bureau of Economic Research.

53   Kraft, M.A., and Papay, J.P. (2014). Can professional environments promote teacher development? Explaining heterogeneity in returns to teaching experience. *Educational Evaluation and Policy Analysis*, 36(4), 476–500.

54   Or have no data available.

55   National Audit Office (2016). *Training New Teachers* (NAO Report by the Comptroller and Auditor General). London: NAO.

56   Allen, R., Belfield, C., Greaves, E., Sharp, C., and Walker, M. (2016). *The longer-term costs and benefits of different initial teacher training routes.* IFS report R118.

57   Department for Education (2017). *School workforce in England: November 2016*, Statistical First Release 25/2017.

58   Sims, S. (2018). *What happens when you pay shortage subject teachers more money? Simulating the effect of early-career salary supplements on teacher supply in England.* London: Gatsby.

59   The pupil population is set to rise by 9 per cent between 2017 and 2026. See: Department for Education (2017). *National pupil projections: July 2017*, Statistical First Release 31/2017.

     Worth, J., Bamford, S., and Durbin, B. (2015). *Should I stay or should I go? NFER analysis of teachers joining and leaving the profession.* Slough, UK: NFER.

60   National Audit Office (2016). *Training New Teachers* (NAO Report by the Comptroller and Auditor General). London: NAO.

61   Johnson, S., Cooper, C., Cartwright, S., Donald, I., Taylor, P. J., and Millet, C. (2005). The experience of work-related stress across occupations. *Journal of Managerial Psychology*, 20(2), 178–187.

62   Ronfeldt, M., Loeb, S., and Wyckoff, J. (2012). How teacher turnover harms student achievement. *American Educational Research Journal*, 50(1) 4–36.

     Atteberry, A., Loeb, S., and Wyckoff, J. (2016). Teacher churning: Reassignment rates and implications for student achievement. *Educational Evaluation and Policy Analysis*, 20(10), 1–28.

     See also: Borg, J.R., Borg, M.O. Stranahan, H.A. (2012). Closing the achievement gap between high-poverty schools and low-poverty schools. *Research in Business and Economics Journal*, 5(March 2012), 1–24.

63   Ronfeldt, M., Loeb, S., and Wyckoff, J. (2012). How teacher turnover harms student achievement. *American Educational Research Journal*, 50(1) 4–36.

64   Hanushek, E.A., Kain, J.F., and Rivkin, S.G. (2004). Why public schools lose teachers. *Journal of Human Resources*, 39(2), 326–354.

65   Allen, R., Burgess, S. and Mayo, J. (2018) The teacher labour market, teacher turnover and disadvantaged schools: new evidence for England. *Education Economics*, 26(1), 4–23.

66   Johnson, S.M., Kraft, M.A., and Papay, J.P. (2012). How context matters in high-need schools: The effects of teachers' working conditions on their professional satisfaction and their students' achievement. *Teachers College Record*, 114(10), 1–39.

67   Boyd, D., Grossman, P., Ing, M., Lankford, H., Loeb, S., and Wyckoff, J. (2010). The influence of school administrators on teacher retention decisions. *American Educational Research Journal*, 48(2), 303–333.

Kukla-Acevedo, S. (2009). Leavers, movers, and stayers: The role of workplace conditions in teacher mobility decisions. *The Journal of Educational Research*, 102(6), 443–452.

68   Sims, S. (2017). *TALIS 2013: Working Conditions, Teacher Job Satisfaction and Retention*. London: Department for Education Statistical Working Paper.

Ladd, H.F. (2011). Teachers' perceptions of their working conditions: How predictive of planned and actual teacher movement? *Educational Evaluation and Policy Analysis*, 33(2), 235–261.

Boyd, D., Grossman, P., Ing, M., Lankford, H., Loeb, S., and Wyckoff, J. (2011). The influence of school administrators on teacher retention decisions. *American Educational Research Journal*, 48(2), 303–333.

Kraft, M.A., and Papay, J.P. (2014). Can professional environments in schools promote teacher development? Explaining heterogeneity in returns to teaching experience. *Educational Evaluation and Policy Analysis*, 36(4), 476–500.

Allen, R., and Sims, S. (2017). *Improving science teacher retention*. London: Wellcome Foundation.

69   Johnson, S.M., and Birkeland, S.E. (2003). Pursuing a 'sense of success': New teachers explain their career decisions. *American Educational Research Journal*, 40(3), 581–617.

70   Private correspondence with Nick Hassey at Teach First.

71   Allen, R., and Sims, S. (2017). *Stress and well-being during initial teacher training*. Unpublished manuscript.

72   Donaldson, M.L., and Johnson, S.M. (2010). The price of mis-assignment: The role of teaching assignments in Teach for America teachers' exit from low-income schools and the teaching profession. *Educational Evaluation and Policy Analysis*, 32(2), 299–323.

73   Demerouti, E., Bakker, A.B., Nachreiner, F., and Schaufeli, W.B. (2001). The job demands-resources model of burnout. *Journal of Applied Psychology*, 86(3), 499–512.

74   Crawford, E.R., Lepine, J.A., and Rich, B.L. (2010). Linking job demands and resources to employee engagement and burnout: A theoretical extension and meta-analytic test. *Journal of Applied Psychology*, 95(5), 834–848.

75   *ibid.*

76   Saks, A.M. (2006). Antecedents and consequences of employee engagement. *Journal of Managerial Psychology*, 21(7), 600–619.

      Harter, J.K., Schmidt, F.L., and Hayes, T.L. (2002). Business-unit-level relationship between employee satisfaction, employee engagement, and business outcomes: A meta-analysis. *Journal of Applied Psychology*, 87(2), 268–279.

      Kim, J., Youngs, P., and Frank, K. (2017). Burnout contagion: Is it due to early career teachers' social networks or organisational exposure? *Teaching and Teacher Education*, 66, 250–260.

77   Hobby, R., and Salt, T. (2016, 27 Feb). The seven deadly sins of executive headship, *Schools Week*. Retrieved from: http://schoolsweek.co.uk/the-seven-deadly-sins-of-executive-headship/.

78   Kraft, M.A., and Papay, J.P. (2014). Can professional environments in schools promote teacher development? Explaining heterogeneity in returns to teaching experience. *Educational Evaluation and Policy Analysis*, 36(4), 476–500.

79   Allen, R. Mian, E., and Sims, S. (2016). *Are there social inequalities in access to high quality teachers?* [Social Market Foundation report]. London: SMF.

80   Andrews, S.P., Gilbert, L.S., and Martin, E.P. (2007). The first years of teaching: Disparities in perceptions of support. *Action in Teacher Education*, 28(4), 4–13.

81   Fernet, C., Guay, F., Senécal, C., and Austin, S. (2012). Predicting intraindividual changes in teacher burnout: The role of perceived

school environment and motivational factors. *Teaching and Teacher Education*, 28(4), 514–525.

82   There were 33,200 trainees starting teacher training in 2015/2016, but only around 24,000 will enter a state-maintained school as a newly qualified teacher. Some will not qualify; others will decide not to teach or to teach in the private sector or overseas. A minority will seek jobs but fail to find an appointment. See: National Audit Office (2016). *Training New Teachers* (NAO Report by the Comptroller and Auditor General). London: NAO.

83   Akerlof, G. (2014). *George A. Akerlof – Biographical. Nobelprize.org.* Retrieved from: www.nobelprize.org/nobel_prizes/economic-sciences/laureates/2001/akerlof-bio.html.

84   Akerlof, G. (1970). The market for lemons: Quality uncertainty and the market mechanism. *Quarterly Journal of Economics*, 84(3), 488–500.

85   Rockoff, J.E., Jacob, B.A., Kane, T.J., and Staiger, D.O. (2011). Can you recognize an effective teacher when you recruit one? *Education Finance and Policy*, 6(1), 43–74.

Hanushek, E.A. (1997). Assessing the effects of school resources on student performance: An update. *Educational Evaluation and Policy Analysis*, 19(2), 141–164.

Goe, L. (2007). *The link between teacher quality and student outcomes: A research synthesis* [Report]. Washington, DC: National Comprehensive Center for Teacher Quality. Retrieved from: www.ncctq.org/publications/LinkBetweenTQandStudentOutcomes.pdf.

Schools in the US are now experimenting with using teacher effectiveness data to inform hiring decisions. See: Cannata, M., Rubin, M., Goldring, E., Grissom, J.A., Nrumerski, C.M., Drake, T.A., and Schuermann, P. (2017). Using teacher effectiveness data for information-rich hiring. *Educational Administration Quarterly*, 53(2), 180–222.

86   Taylor, E.S. (forthcoming). Skills, job tasks, and productivity in teaching: Evidence from a randomized trial of instruction practices. *Journal of Labor Economics*, 36(3).

87   Engel, M. (2013). Problematic preferences? A mixed method examination of what principals' preference for teacher characteristics in Chicago. *Educational Administration Quarterly*, 49, 52–91.

88   Loeb, S., Kalogrides, D., and Béteille, T. (2012). Effective schools: Teacher hiring, assignment, development, and retention. *Education Finance and Policy*, 7, 269–304.

Engel, M. (2013). Problematic preferences? A mixed method examination of what principals' preference for teacher characteristics in Chicago. *Educational Administration Quarterly*, 49, 52–91.

Ralph, E.G., Kesten, C., Lang, H., and Smith, D. (1998). Hiring new teachers: What do school districts look for? *Journal of Teacher Education*, 49, 47–56.

Cannata, M., and Engel, M. (2012). Does charter status determine preferences? Comparing the hiring preferences of charter and traditional public school principals. *Education Finance and Policy*, 7, 455–488.

89   We reference this literature elsewhere in the book. For a UK perspective on how this has changed their use in schools, blogger David Didau has written multiple posts. As a starting point we recommend: Didau, D. (2015, 16 September). *Why sacrificing chickens will not help us evaluate teachers' performance* [Blog post]. Retrieved from: www.learningspy.co.uk/leadership/why-sacrificing-chickens-will-not-help-us-evaluate-teachers-performance/.

90   Kane, T., and Staiger, D. (2005). *Using imperfect information to identify effective teachers* [Unpublished manuscript]. Retrieved from: www.dartmouth.edu/~dstaiger/Papers/2005/Kane%20Staiger%20tea cher%20quality%204%2028%2005.pdf.

91   Department for Education (2012, 13 January). *Schools get more freedom to manage teacher performance* [Press release]. Retrieved from: www.gov.uk/government/news/schools-get-more-freedom-to-manage-teacher-performance.

92   Feng, L., and Sass, T. (2017). Teacher quality and teacher mobility, *Education Finance and Policy*, 12(3), 396–418.

93   Burgess, S., Greaves, E., and Murphy, R. (2017). *Evaluation of teachers' pay reform (technical appendix)* [DfE Research Report]. Retrieved from: www.gov.uk/government/uploads/system/uploads/attachment_data/file/652765/Evaluation_of_Teachers_Pay_Reform_-_Technical_Appendix.pdf.

94   Also, initial teacher training institutions have long been incentivised by Ofsted to pass inadequate trainees since they are judged on their pass rates.

95   Jacob, B.A., and Lefgren, L. (2008). Can principals identify effective teachers? Evidence on subjective performance evaluation in education. *Journal of Labor Economics*, 26(1), 101–136.

96   Department for Education (2016). *Initial Teacher Training census for the academic year 2016 to 2017, England* [Statistical First

Release 57/2016]. Retrieved from: www.gov.uk/government/uploads/
system/uploads/attachment_data/file/572290/ITT_Census_1617_SFR_
Final.pdf.

97   Pye, J., Stobart, R., and Lindley, L. (2016). *Newly Qualified Teachers:
Annual survey 2016* [NCTL Research report August 2016]. Retrieved
from: www.gov.uk/government/uploads/system/uploads/attachment_
data/file/570147/NQT2016_National_Survey_FINAL.pdf.

98   Worth, J. (2017). *Teacher retention and turnover research – Research
update 2: Teacher dynamics in Multi-Academy Trusts*, NFER Research
Report (June 2017).

99   Sims, S. and Allen, R. (2018). Identifying schools with high usage and
high loss of Newly Qualified Teachers. *National Institute Economic
Review*, 243(1), R27–R36.

100   Spielgelhalter, D. (2005). Funnel plots for comparing institutional
performance. *Statistics in Medicine*, 24, 1185–1202.

101   See, for example, the news stories on this website: www.legalweek.
com/tag/retention.

102   Dee, T. (2012). *School turnarounds: Evidence from the 2009 stimulus*
(NBER WP No.17990). Cambridge, MA: National Bureau of Economic
Research.

103   Allen, R., Bibby, D., Parameshwaran, M., and Nye, P. (2016). Linking
ITT and workforce data: (Initial Teacher Training Performance Profiles
and School Workforce Census), NCTL Research Report July 2016.

104   McGill, R. (2014, 14 June). *Defunct? The role of observations at
interview* [Blog post]. Retrieved from: www.teachertoolkit.co.uk/
2014/06/14/defunct-the-role-of-observations-at-interview-by-
teachertoolkit.

105   Johnson, S.M., and Birkeland, S.E. (2003). Pursuing a "sense of
success": New teachers explain their career decisions. *American
Educational Research Journal*, 40(3), 581–617.

106   YouGov (2015). *NUT-YouGov teacher survey results*. Retrieved from:
www.teachers.org.uk/files/nut-yougov-teacher-survey-results-
pr167–2015.xlsx.

107   Department for Education (2017). *School workforce in England:
November 2016*. Retrieved from: www.gov.uk/government/statistics/
school-workforce-in-england-november-2016.

108   Gillard, D. (2011). *Education in England: a brief history* [Online
book]. Retrieved from: www.educationengland.org.uk/history.

109   Williams, R. (1961). *The Long Revolution*. London: Chatto & Windus.

110   Bourne, R., and MacArthur, B. (1970). *The struggle for education 1870–1970*. London: Schoolmaster.

111   Kingsford, P. (1987). Chapter 2: Born to be daily labourers 1840–1870. In P. Kingsford (ed.), *North Mymms schools and their children: 1700–1964*. Retrieved from: www.brookmans.com/history/kingsford3/ch2.shtml.

112   Department for Education (2013, 4 September). *New pay policies reward best teachers* [Online news]. Retrieved from: www.gov.uk/government/news/new-pay-policies-reward-best-teachers.

113   Sharp, C., Walker, M., Lynch, S., Puntan, L., Bernardinelli, D., Worth, J. Greaves, E., Burgess, S., and Murphy, R. (2017). *Evaluation of Teachers' Pay Reform: Final Report*. Retrieved from: www.gov.uk/government/publications/teachers-pay-reform-evaluation.

114   The work of the MET Project suggests we can identify our best and worst teachers somewhat reliably by combining measures of pupil test score growth, observations of teaching and student surveys. Arguably, 'somewhat' is not sufficiently precise to operate a performance-based pay system!

115   Imberman, S. (2015). How effective are financial incentives for teachers? *IZA World of Labor* 2015(158). doi: 10.15185/izawol.158.

      Podgursky, M., and Springer M. (2007). Teacher performance pay: A review. *Journal of Policy Analysis and Management*, 26(4), 909–949.

116   Hasnain, Z., Manning, N., and Pierskalla, J. (2012). *Performance-related pay in the public sector: A review of theory and evidence* (policy research working paper 6043, April 2012). New York: The World Bank.

      Ray, K., Foley, B., Tsang, T., Walne, D., and Bajorek, Z. (2014). *A review of the evidence on the impact, effectiveness and value for money of performance – related pay in the public sector*. London: The Work Foundation.

      Weibel, A., Rost, K., and Osterloh, M. (2009). Pay for performance in the public sector – benefits and (hidden) costs. *Journal of Public Administration Research and Theory*, 20, 387–412.

117   Dee, T.S., and Wyckoff, J. (2015). Incentives, selection, and teacher performance: Evidence from IMPACT. *Journal of Policy Analysis and Management*, 34(2), 267–297.

Adnot, M., Dee, T., Katz, V., and Wyckoff, J. (2016). *Teacher turnover, teacher quality, and student achievement in DCPS* (NBER Working Paper No. 21922). Cambridge, MA: National Bureau of Economic Research.

118   Sojourner, A.J., Mykerezi, E., and West, K.L. (2014). Teacher pay reform and productivity panel data evidence from adoptions of Q-Comp in Minnesota. *Journal of Human Resources*, 49(4), 945–981.

119   Lavy, V. (2009). Performance pay and teachers' effort, productivity, and grading ethics. *American Economic Review*, 99(5), 1979–2011.

120   Atkinson, A., Burgess, S., Croxson, B., Gregg, P. Propper, C., Slater, H., and Wilson, D. (2009). Evaluating the impact of performance-related pay for teachers in England. *Labour Economics*, 16(3), 251–261.

121   Springer, M.G., Ballou, D., Hamilton, L.S., Le, V.-N., Lockwood, J.R., McCaffrey, D.F., Pepper, M., and Stecher, B.M. (2012). *Final Report: Experimental Evidence from the Project on Incentives in Teaching (POINT)*. Nashville, TN: National Center on Performance Incentives.

122   Fryer, R.G. (2013). Teacher incentives and student achievement: Evidence from New York City public schools. *Journal of Labor Economics*, 31(2), 373–407.

Goodman, S.F., and Turner, L.J. (2013). The design of teacher incentive pay and educational outcomes: Evidence from the New York City bonus program. *Journal of Labor Economics*, 31(2), 409–420.

123   Glazerman, S., and Seifullah, A. (2012). *An evaluation of the Chicago Teacher Advancement Program (Chicago TAP) after four years (final report)*. Washington, DC: Mathematical Policy Research.

124   Fryer, R.G., Levitt, S.D., List, J.A., and Sadoff, S. (2012). *Enhancing the efficacy of teacher incentives through loss aversion: A field experiment* (NBER Working Paper No. 18237). Cambridge, MA: National Bureau of Economic Research.

125   Grissom, J.A., Kalogrides, D., and Loeb, S. (2017). Strategic staffing? How performance pressures affect the distribution of teachers within schools and resulting student achievement. *American Educational Research Journal*, Online First.

126   Gorman, L. (2003). *Do Incentives Cause Teachers to Cheat?* (NBER Digest July 2003). Retrieved from: www.nber.org/digest/jul03/w9413.html, provides a summary and links to some key economics studies. See also: www.theatlantic.com/education/archive/2016/04/why-teachers-cheat/480039/, for major international perspective. The Guardian Secret Teacher has reported instances of cheating on multiple

occasions, e.g.: www.theguardian.com/teacher-network/2015/jun/27/secret-teacher-we-help-pupils-to-but-how-long-before-its-exposed.

127   McInerney, L. (2017, 29 November). *A startling story on SATs cheating* [Blog post]. Retrieved from: http://teachertapp.co.uk/2017/11/startling-story-sats-cheating/.

128   Chamberlin, R., Wragg, T., Haynes, G., and Wragg, C. (2002). Performance-related pay and the teaching profession: A review of the literature. *Research Papers in Education*, 17(1), 31–49.

      See also Gillard, D. (2011). Chapter 3: 1860–1900 (Class divisions). In *Education in England: A brief history* [Online book]. Retrieved from: www.educationengland.org.uk/history.

129   Frey, B.S. (1992). *Economics as a science of human behaviour. Towards a new social science paradigm*. Boston/Dordrecht/London: Kluwer.

130   Wigfield, A., and Cambria, J. (2010). Expectancy-value theory: Retrospective and prospective. In T.C. Urdan and S.A. Karabenick (eds), *The decade ahead: Theoretical perspectives on motivation and achievement (advances in motivation and achievement, volume 16 part A)* (pp. 35–70). Bingley, UK: Emerald.

131   Richardson, P.W., and Watt, H.M.G. (2014). Why people choose teaching as a career: An expectancy-value approach to understanding teacher motivation. In P.W. Richardson, S.A. Karabenick and H.M.G. Watt (eds), *Teacher motivation: Theory and practice* (pp. 3–19). New York: Routledge.

132   Parker, P.D., Martin, A.J., Colmar, S., and Liem, G.A. (2012). Teachers' workplace well-being: Exploring a process model of goal orientation, coping behavior, engagement, and burnout. *Teaching and Teacher Education*, 28(4), 503–513.

133   On turnover: Richer, S.F., Blanchard, C., and Vallerand, R.J. (2002). A motivational model of work turnover. *Journal of Applied Social Psychology*, 32(10), 2089–2113.

      Reviews:

      Patall, E.A., Cooper, H., and Robinson, J.C. (2008). The effects of choice on intrinsic motivation and related outcomes: A meta-analysis of research findings. *Psychological Bulletin*, 134(2), 270–300.

      Ryan, R., and Deci, E. (2000). Intrinsic and extrinsic motivations: Classic definitions and new directions. *Contemporary Educational Psychology*, 25, 54–67.

Deci, E.L., and Ryan, R.M. (2013). The importance of universal psychological needs for understanding motivation in the workplace. In M. Gagné (ed.), *The Oxford handbook of work engagement, motivation, and self-determination theory*. Oxford, UK: Oxford University Press.

134   Taylor, I.M., Ntoumanis, N., and Standage, M. (2008). A self-determination theory approach to understanding the antecedents of teachers' motivational strategies in physical education. *Journal of Sport and Exercise Psychology*, 30, 75–94.

Pelletier, L.G., Séguin-Lévesque, C., and Legault, L. (2002). Pressure from above and pressure from below as determinants of teachers' motivation and teaching behaviors. *Journal of Educational Psychology*, 94(February), 186–196.

Eyal, O., and Roth, G. (2011). Principals' leadership and teachers' motivation: Self-determination theory analysis. *Journal of Educational Administration*, 49(3), 256–275.

Reeve, J., and Su, Y.-L. (2013). Teacher motivation. In M. Gagné (ed.), *The Oxford handbook of work engagement, motivation, and self-determination theory*. Oxford, UK: Oxford University Press.

Chiong, C., Menzies, L., and Parameshwaran, M. (2017). Why do long-serving teachers stay in the teaching profession? Analysing the motivations of teachers with 10 or more years' experience in England, *British Educational Research Journal*, forthcoming.

135   Ryan, R., and Deci, E. (2000). Intrinsic and extrinsic motivations: Classic definitions and new directions. *Contemporary Educational Psychology*, 25, 54–67.

136   Gagne, M., and Deci, E.L. (2013). Self-determination theory and work motivation. *Journal of Organizational Behavior*, 26(4), 331–362.

Ryan, R., and Deci, E. (2000). Intrinsic and extrinsic motivations: Classic definitions and new directions. *Contemporary Educational Psychology*, 25, 54–67.

137   Cameron, J., Banko, K. M., and Pierce, W. D. (2001). Pervasive negative effects of rewards on intrinsic motivation: The myth continues. *The Behavior Analyst*, 24(1), 1–44.

Deci, E.L., Koestner, R., and Ryan, R.M. (1999). A meta-analytic review of experiments examining the effects of extrinsic rewards on intrinsic motivation. *Psychological Bulletin*, 125(6), 627–668.

138   Grolnick, W.S., and Ryan, R.M. (1989). Parent styles associated with children's self-regulation and competence in school. *Journal of Educational Psychology*, 81(2), 143–154.

Sheldon, K.M., and Elliot, A.J. (1998). Not all personal goals are personal: Comparing autonomous and controlled reasons for goals as predictors of effort and attainment. *Personality and Social Psychology*, 24(5), 546–557.

Sheldon, K.M., and Krieger, L.S. (2007). Understanding the negative effects of legal education on law students: A longitudinal test of self-determination theory. *Personality and Social Psychology Bulletin*, 33(6), 883–897.

139   Williams, G.C., Grow, V.M., Freedman, Z.R., Ryan, R.M., and Deci, E.L. (1996). Motivational predictors of weight loss and weight-loss maintenance. *Journal of Personality and Social Psychology*, 70(1), 115–126.

140   Williams, G.C., McGregor, H., Sharp, D., Kouides, R.W., Lévesque, C.S., Ryan, R.M., and Deci, E.L. (2006). A self-determination multiple risk intervention trial to improve smokers' health. *Journal of General Internal Medicine*, 21(12), 1288–1294.

141   Pelletier, L.G., Fortier, M.S., Vallerand R.J., and Briere, N.M. (2001). Associations among perceived autonomy support, forms of self-regulation, and persistence: A prospective study. *Motivation and Emotion*, 25(4), 279–306.

142   Cerasoli, C.P., Nicklin, J.M., and Ford, M.T. (2014). Intrinsic motivation and extrinsic incentives jointly predict perform-ance: A 40-year meta-analysis. *Psychological Bulletin*, 140(4), 980–1008.

Cerasoli, C.P., Nicklin, J.M. and Nassrelrgrgawi, A.S. (2016). Perform-ance, incentives, and needs for autonomy, competence, and relatedness: a meta-analysis. *Motivation and Emotion*, 40(6) 781–813.

143   Banerjee, N., Stearns, E. Moller, S., and Mickelson, R.A. (2017). Teacher job satisfaction and student achievement: The roles of teacher professional community and teacher collaboration in schools. *American Journal of Education*, 123(2).

144   Roth, G. (2011). Antecedents of teachers' autonomy-supportive behaviour. Paper presented at the 14th Biennial conference of the European Association for Research in Learning and Instruction (EARLI), Exeter, UK.

Gagné, M., and Deci, E. L. (2005). Self-determination theory and work motivation. *Journal of Organizational behavior*, 26(4), 331–362.

Sheldon, K. M., Turban, D. B., Brown, K. G., Barrick, M. R., and Judge, T. A. (2003). Applying self-determination theory to organizational research. *Research in Personnel and Human Resources Management*, 22, 357–393.

Eyal, O., and Roth, G. (2011). Principals' leadership and teachers' motivation: Self-determination theory analysis. *Journal of Educational Administration*, 49(3), 256–275.

Sims, S. (2017). TALIS 2013: *Working Conditions, Teacher Job Satisfaction and Retention*, Department for Education Research Paper. Retrieved from: www.gov.uk/government/uploads/system/uploads/attachment_data/file/656249/TALIS_2013_Evidence_on_Working_Conditions_Teacher_Job_Satisfaction_and_Retention_Nov_2017.pdf.

145   Heathfield Community College (2017). *Heathfield teach share blog* [Website]. Retrieved from: https://heathfieldteachshare.wordpress.com.

146   Enser, M. (2017, 26 June). *Feeling blue about the state of teaching? Here are reasons to be optimistic.* Retrieved from: www.theguardian.com/teacher-network/teacher-blog/2017/jun/26/reasons-optimistic-teaching-funding-cuts.

147   Ronfeldt, M., Owens Farmer, S., and McQueen, K. (2015). Teacher collaboration in instructional teams and student achievement. *American Educational Research Journal*, 52 (3), 475–514.

148   Quigley, A. (2014, 8 March). *Teacher burnout* [Blog post]. Retrieved from: www.theconfidentteacher.com/2014/03/teacher-burnout.

149   Steinberg, M.P., and Garrett, R. (2016). Classroom composition and measured teacher performance: What do teacher observation scores really measure? *Educational Evaluation and Policy Analysis*, 38(2), 293–317.

150   Jackson, C.K. (2016). *What do test scores miss? The importance of teacher effects on non-test score outcomes*, Institute for Policy Research Northwestern University working paper 16–03. Retrieved from: www.ipr.northwestern.edu/publications/docs/workingpapers/2016/WP-16-03.pdf.

151   Bill and Melinda Gates Foundation (2009, November). *Foundation commits $335 million to promote effective teaching and raise student achievement* [Press release]. Retrieved from: www.gatesfoundation.org/Media-Center/Press-Releases/2009/11/Foundation-Commits-$335-Million-to-Promote-Effective-Teaching-and-Raise-Student-Achievement.

152   Bryan, W.L., and Harter, N. (1899). Studies on the telegraphic language: The acquisition of a hierarchy of habits. *Psychology Review*, 6, 345–75.

153   Ericsson, K.A. (2002). Attaining excellence through deliberate practice: Insights from the study of expert performance. *Teaching and Learning: The Essential Readings*, 4–37.

154   For an early formulation of the definition of deliberate practice, see: Ericsson, K.A., Krampe, R.T., and Tesch-Römer, C. (1993). The role of deliberate practice in the acquisition of expert performance. *Psychological Review*, 100(3), 363.

      For a clearer, more recent version, see page 72 of: Ericsson, K.A. (2004). Deliberate practice and the acquisition and maintenance of expert performance in medicine and related domains. *Academic Medicine*, 79(10), S70–S81.

155   Ericsson, K.A., Krampe, R.T., and Tesch-Römer, C. (1993). The role of deliberate practice in the acquisition of expert performance. *Psychological Review*, 100(3), 363.

156   Charness, N., Tuffiash, M., Krampe, R., Reingold, E., and Vasyukova, E. (2005). The role of deliberate practice in chess expertise. *Applied Cognitive Psychology*, 19(2), 151–65.

157   Krampe, R.T., and Ericsson, K.A. (1996). Maintaining excellence: Deliberate practice and elite performance in young and older pianists. *Journal of Experimental Psychology: General*, 125(4), 331–359.

158   Keith, N., and Ericsson, K.A. (2007). A deliberate practice account of typing proficiency in everyday typists. *Journal of Experimental Psychology: Applied*, 13(3), 134–45.

159   Ericsson, K.A. (2006). The influence of experience and deliberate practice on the development of superior expert performance. In K.A. Ericsson, N. Charness, P.J. Feltovich and R.R. Hoffman (eds), *The Cambridge handbook of expertise and expert performance*. Cambridge, UK: Cambridge University Press, 683–704.

160   Hambrick, D.Z., Oswald, F.L., Altmann, E.M., Meinz, E.J., Gobet, F., and Campitelli, G. (2014). Deliberate practice: Is that all it takes to become an expert? *Intelligence*, 45, 34–45.

161   Ericsson, K.A. (2004). Deliberate practice and the acquisition and maintenance of expert performance in medicine and related domains. *Academic Medicine*, 79(10), 70–81.

162   Ericsson, K.A., Whyte, I.V., and Ward, P. (2007). Expert performance in nursing: Reviewing research on expertise in nursing within the

framework of the expert-performance approach. *Advances in Nursing Science*, 30(1), 58–71.

163 Kirkman, M.A. (2013). Deliberate practice, domain-specific expertise, and implications for surgical education in current climes. *Journal of Surgical Education*, 70(3), 309–17.

164 Price, J., Naik, V., Boodhwani, M., Brandys, M., Hendry, P., and Lam, B.K. (2011). A randomized evaluation of simulation training on performance of vascular anastomosis on a high-fidelity in vivo model: The role of deliberate practice. *The Journal of Thoracic and Cardiovascular Surgery*, 142(3), 496–503.

165 McGaghie, W.C., Issenberg, S.B., Cohen, M.E.R., Barsuk, J.H., and Wayne, D.B. (2011). Does simulation-based medical education with deliberate practice yield better results than traditional clinical education? A meta-analytic comparative review of the evidence. *Academic Medicine: Journal of the Association of American Medical Colleges*, 86(6), 706–711.

166 Didau, D. (2015). *What if everything you thought about teaching was wrong*. Carmarthen, UK: Crown.

167 Coe, R. (2013). *Improving education: A triumph of hope over experience*, Inaugural lecture of Professor Rob Coe, Durham University. Retrieved from: www.cem.org/attachments/publications/ImprovingEducation2013.pdf.

168 Wiliam, D. (2011). *Embedded formative assessment*. Bloomington, IN: Solution Tree Press.

169 Mihaly, K., McCaffrey, D.F., Staiger, D.O., and Lockwood, J.R. (2013). A composite estimator of effective teaching, measures of effective teaching (MET) report: Bill and Melinda Gates Foundation. Retrieved from: http://k12education.gatesfoundation.org/resource/a-composite-estimator-of-effective-teaching/.

170 Strong, M., Gargani, J., and Hacifazlioglu, O. (2011). Do we know a successful teacher when we see one? Experiments in the identification of effective teachers. *Journal of Teacher Education*, 62(4) 367–382.

171 Wiliam, D. (2007). Changing classroom practice. *Educational Leadership*, 65(4), 36–42.

Rowe, M. (1986). Wait time: Slowing down may be a way of speeding up! *Journal of Teacher Education*, 37(1), 43–50.

172 Webb, T.L., and Sheeran, P. (2006). Does changing behavioral intentions engender behavior change? A meta-analysis of the experimental evidence. *Psychological Bulletin*, 132(2), 249–268.

173   Wood, W.. and Neal, D.T. (2007). A new look at habits and the habit-goal interface. *Psychological Review*, 114(4), 843.

Nilsen, P., Roback, K., Broström, A., and Ellström, P.E. (2012). Creatures of habit: Accounting for the role of habit in implementation research on clinical behaviour change. *Implementation Science*, 7(1), 53.

Schwabe, L., and Wolf, O.T. (2010). Socially evaluated cold pressor stress after instrumental learning favors habits over goal-directed action. *Psychoneuroendocrinology*, 35(7), 977–986.

174   Wiliam, D. (2007). Changing classroom practice. *Educational Leadership*, 65(4), 36–42.

175   Johnson, S., Cooper, C., Cartwright, S., Donald, I., Taylor, P.J., and Millet, C. (2005). The experience of work-related stress across occupations. *Journal of Managerial Psychology*, 20(2), 178–187.

176   Seger, C.A., and Spiering, B.J. (2011). A critical review of habit learning and the Basal Ganglia. *Frontiers in Systems Neuroscience*, 5, 66.

177   Jovanovic, B., and Nyarko, Y. (1995). A Bayesian learning model fitted to a variety of empirical learning curves. *Brookings Papers on Economic Activity. Microeconomics*, 247–305.

178   Bryan, W.L., and Harter, N. (1899). Studies on the telegraphic language: The acquisition of a hierarchy of habits. *Psychology Review*, 6, 345–375.

179   Fletcher-Wood, H. (2016, 24 April). *Using exit tickets to assess and plan: 'The tuning fork of teaching'* [Blog post]. Retrieved from: https://improvingteaching.co.uk/2016/04/24/exit-tickets-assess-plan/.

180   Ng, J.Y., Ntoumanis, N., Thøgersen-Ntoumani, C., Deci, E.L., Ryan, R.M., Duda, J.L., and Williams, G.C. (2012). Self-determination theory applied to health contexts: A meta-analysis. *Perspectives on Psychological Science*, 7(4), 325–340.

Koestner, R., Horberg, E.J., Gaudreau, P., Powers, T., Di Dio, P., Bryan, C., Jochum, R., and Salter, N. (2006). Bolstering implementation plans for the long haul: The benefits of simultaneously boosting self-concordance or self- efficacy. *Personality and Social Psychology Bulletin*, 32, 1547–1558.

181   Webb, T.L., and Sheeran, P. (2006). Does changing behavioral intentions engender behavior change? A meta-analysis of the experimental evidence. *Psychological Bulletin*, 132(2), 249–268.

See also:

Hagger, M.S., Luszczynska, A., de Wit, J., Benyamini, Y., Burkert, S., Chamberland, P.E., and Gauchet, A. (2016). Implementation intention and planning interventions in health psychology: Recommendations from the synergy expert group for research and practice. *Psychology and Health*, 31(7), 814–839.

182   Denrell, J., and March, J. G. (2001). Adaptation as information restriction: The hot stove effect. *Organization Science*, 12(5), 523–538.

183   For more information on Teacher Learner Communities see, for example, www.dylanwiliamcenter.com/professional-development/. Lesson Study is being supported in England by the Teacher Development Trust: http://tdtrust.org/what-is-lesson-study.

184   Kraft, M.A., Blazar, D. and Hogan, D. (2018) The Effect of Teacher Coaching on Instruction and Achievement: A Meta-Analysis of the Causal Evidence, *Review of Educational Research*. First published February 22, 2018 at https://doi.org/10.3102/0034654318759268.

185   Defined as intervention in which an instructional expert provides individualised feedback, at least every two weeks, over a sustained period of time, on specific techniques which are directly relevant to the teachers' classroom practice.

Kraft, M.A., Blazar, D. and Hogan, D. (2018) The Effect of Teacher Coaching on Instruction and Achievement: A Meta-Analysis of the Causal Evidence, *Review of Educational Research*. First published February 22, 2018 at https://doi.org/10.3102/0034654318759268.

186   Sonesh, S.C., Coultas, C.W., Lacerenza, C.N., Shannon, L., Benishek, L.E., and Salas, E. (2015). The power of coaching: A meta-analytic investigation. *Coaching*, 8(2), 73–95.

Kretlow, A.G., and Bartholomew, C.C. (2010). Using coaching to improve the fidelity of evidence-based practices: A review of studies. *Teacher Education and Special Education: The Journal of the Teacher Education Division of the Council for Exceptional Children*, 33(4), 279–299.

Grant, A.M. (2014). Autonomy support, relationship satisfaction and goal focus in the coach–coachee relationship: Which best predicts coaching success? *Coaching: An International Journal of Theory, Research and Practice*, 7(1), 18–38.

187   Higgins, S., Kokotsaki, D., and Coe, R. (2012). *Teaching and learning toolkit: Technical appendices*, Educational Endowment Foundation report.

188   Allen, J., Gregory, A., Mikami, A., Lun, J., Hamre, B., and Pianta, R. (2013). Observations of effective teacher-student interactions in secondary school classrooms: Predicting student achievement with the classroom assessment scoring system-secondary. *School Psychology Review*, 42(1), 76.

Kane, T.J., and Staiger, D.O. (2012). Gathering feedback for teaching: Combining high-quality observations with student surveys and achievement gains. *Education, January* 1–68. Retrieved from: http://metproject.org/downloads/MET_Gathering_Feedback_Research_Paper.pdf.

189   Allen, J.P., Hafen, C.A., Gregory, A.C., Mikami, A.Y., and Pianta, R. (2015). Enhancing secondary school instruction and student achievement: Replication and extension of the My Teaching Partner-Secondary Intervention. *Journal of Research on Educational Effectiveness*, 8(4), 475–489.

Allen, J.P., Pianta, R.C., Gregory, A., Mikami, A.Y. and Lun, J. (2011). An interaction-based approach to enhancing secondary school instruction and student achievement. *Science*, 333(6045), 1034–1037.

190   Deans for Impact (2016). *Practice with purpose: The emerging science of teacher expertise*. Austin, TX: Deans for Impact.

191   Grant, A.M., and Hartley, M. (2013). Developing the leader as coach: Insights, strategies and tips for embedding coaching skills in the workplace. *Coaching: An International Journal of Theory, Research and Practice*, 6(2), 102–115.

192   McInerney, L. (2017, 6 November). *What teachers tapped this week* [Blog post]. Retrieved from: http://teachertapp.co.uk/2017/11/teachers-tapped-week-8/.

193   Gibson, S., Oliver, L., and Dennison, M. (2015). *Workload challenge: Analysis of teacher consultation responses* (Research Report DfE-RR445). London: Department for Education.

194   TNS BMRB (2014). *Teachers' workload diary survey 2013* (Research Report DfE-RR316). London: Department for Education. Figure 6.

195   PricewaterhouseCoopers (2001). *Teacher Workload Study*. London: Department for Education and Skills.

196   Bubb, S., and Earley P. (2004). *Managing teacher workload: Work-life balance and wellbeing*, London: SAGE.

197   *ibid.*

198   Deakin, G., James, N., Tickner, M., and Tidswell, J. (2010). *Teachers' workload diary survey 2010* (Research Report DfE-RR057). London: Department for Education.

199   Highton, J., Leonardi, S., Richards, N., Choudhoury, A., Sofroniou, N., and Owen, D. (2017). *Teacher Workload Survey 2016* (DfE research report RR633). London: Department for Education.

200   Gibson, S., Oliver, L., and Dennison, M. (2015). *Workload challenge: Analysis of teacher consultation responses* (Research Report DfE-RR445). London: Department for Education.

201   Kirby, J. (2013, 30 March). *What can we learn from Dylan Wiliam and AfL?* [Blog post]. Retrieved from: https://pragmaticreform. wordpress.com/2013/03/30/afl.

202   McInerney, L. (2017, 6 November). *What teachers tapped this week* [Blog post]. Retrieved from: http://teachertapp.co.uk/2017/11/ teachers-tapped-week-8.

203   Hendrick, C., and Macpherson, R. (2017). *What does this look like in the classroom?* Woodbridge, UK: John Catt.

204   Netflix's CEO Reed Hastings (with Patty McCord) describes this culture in detail in an excellent presentation: *A Reference Guide on Netflix's Freedom and Responsibility Culture.* Retrieved from: https://hbr.org/2014/01/how-netflix-reinvented-hr.

205   McInerney, L. (2017, 23 October). *What Teachers Tapped This Week #6* [Blog post]. Retrieved from: http://teachertapp.co.uk/2017/10/ week-findings-22nd-october-2017.

206   Ingvarson, L., Kleinhenz, E., Beavis, A., Barwick, H., Carthy, I., and Wilkinson, J. (2005). *Secondary teacher workload study: report* (ACER Report). Retrieved from ACER website: http://research.acer.edu.au/ workforce/2.

207   In the OECD's Teaching and Learning in Schools (TALIS) study in 2013, country average reported working hours is uncorrelated with whether teachers agree that teaching is advantageous.

208   Moller, A. C., Deci, E. L., and Ryan, R. M. (2006). Choice and ego-depletion: The moderating role of autonomy. *Personality and Social Psychology Bulletin,* 32(8), 1024–1036.

       Ryan, R. M., and Frederick, C. (1997). On energy, personality, and health: Subjective vitality as a dynamic reflection of well-being. *Journal of Personality,* 65(3), 529–565.

209   PricewaterhouseCoopers (2001). *Teacher workload study.* London: Department for Education and Skills.

210   Department for Education (2016). *Reducing teacher workload* [Poster]. Retrieved from: www.gov.uk/government/uploads/system/uploads/ attachment_data/file/593913/6.2799_DFE_MB_Reducing_Teacher_ Workload_Poster_20161213_print.pdf.

211   DiMaggio, P.J., and Powell, W.W. (1983). The iron cage revisited: Institutional isomorphism and collective rationality in organizational fields. *American Sociological Review*, 48(2), 147–160.

212   TNS BMRB (2014). *Teachers' workload diary survey 2013* (Research Report DfE-RR316). London: Department for Education.

Gibson, S., Oliver, L., and Dennison, M. (2015). *Workload challenge: Analysis of teacher consultation responses* (Research Report DfE-RR445). London: Department for Education.

213   For an example of this process with reference to 'triple marking', see: Selfridge, R. (2014, 1 December). *The high cost of 'effective feedback' – the triple marking fiasco* [Blog post]. Retrieved from: http://icingonthecakeblog.weebly.com/blog/the-high-cost-of-effective-feedback-the-triple-marking-fiasco.

214   Larson, M.S. (1977). *The rise of professionalism: A sociological analysis*. Berkeley, CA: University of California Press.

Collins, R. (1979). *The credential society*. New York: Academic Press.

215   For a description of these processes in schools, read: Quinn, M. (2017, 16 November). *We can re-build it* [Blog post]. Retrieved from: https://markquinn1968.wordpress.com/2017/11/16/we-can-rebuild-it.

216   Spencer, R. (2017, 12 November). *Teacher workload – should we negotiate more in order to achieve less?* [Blog post]. Retrieved from: http://richardspencer1979.blogspot.co.uk/2017/11/teacher-workload-should-we-negotiate.

217   Ofsted (2017). *Ofsted inspections: myths*. Retrieved from: www.gov.uk/government/publications/school-inspection-handbook-from-september-2015/ofsted-inspections-mythbusting.

218   Many teachers have written wonderful blogs on this topic, including: Newmark, B. (2016, 26 September). *Verbal feedback: Telling them what to do* [Blog post]. Retrieved from: http://bennewmark.edublogs.org/2016/09/26/227.

Enser, M. (2017, 10 October). *Making a fuss of feedback* [Blog post]. Retrieved from: https://teachreal.wordpress.com/2017/10/10/making-a-fuss-of-feedback/amp.

Percival, A. (2017, 28 September). *No Written Marking. Job Done.* [Blog post]. Retrieved from: http://primarypercival.weebly.com/blog/no-written-marking-job-done.

219   Newmark, B. (2017, 23 August). *Make it visible. Don't take work home* [Blog post]. Retrieved from: https://bennewmark.wordpress.com/2017/08/23/dont-take-work-home-make-it-visible.

220   Sherrington, T. (2017, 1 December). 10 low impact activities to do less of – or stop altogether [Blog post]. Retrieved from: https://teacherhead. com/2017/12/01/10-low-impact-activities-to-do-less-of-or-stop-altogether.

221   For a strong justification of this, see Carter, A. (2015). *Carter review of initial teacher training* [Report for Department for Education]. Retrieved from: www.gov.uk/government/publications/carter-review-of-initial-teacher-training.

222   Technically, Arthur Pigou was the first economist to formalise the ideas around general skills and underinvestment in training; Gary Becker simply developed his models further.

223   Becker, G. (1994). *Human capital: A theoretical and empirical analysis with special reference to education* (3rd edition), Chicago, IL: The University of Chicago Press.

224   Acemoglu, D., and Pischke, J.S. (1998). Why Do Firms Train? Theory and Evidence. *The Quarterly Journal of Economics*, 113(1), 79–119.

225   Hendricks, M.D. (2014). Does it pay to pay teachers more? Evidence from Texas. *Journal of Public Economics*, 109, 50–63.

Ransom, M.R., and Sims, D.P. (2010). Estimating the firm's labor supply curve in a "new monopsony" framework: Schoolteachers in Missouri. *Journal of Labor Economics*, 28(2), 331–355.

226   Ward, H. (2017, 4 December). *Teacher apprenticeships: What you need to know* [News article]. Times Educational Supplement. Retrieved from: www.tes.com/news/school-news/breaking-news/teacher-apprenticeships-what-you-need-know.

227   Gregory, A., Ruzek, E., Hafen, C.A., Mikami, A.Y., Allen, J.P., and Pianta, R.C. (2017). My teaching partner-secondary: A video-based coaching model. *Theory into Practice*, 56(1), 38–45. doi.org/10.1080/00405841.2016.1260402

Allen, J.P., Hafen, C.A., Gregory, A.C., Mikami, A.Y., and Pianta, R. (2015). Enhancing secondary school instruction and student achievement: Replication and extension of the my teaching partner-secondary intervention. *Journal of Research on Educational Effectiveness*, 8(4), 475–489.

Allen, J.P., Pianta, R.C., Gregory, A., Mikami, A.Y., and Lun, J. (2011). An interaction-based approach to enhancing secondary school instruction and student achievement. *Science*, 333(6045), 1034–1037. doi.org/10.1126/science.1207998

228   Our proposals bear some similarities to an alternative certification programme in the US:

Gerdeman, R.D., Wan, Y., Molefe, A., Bos, J.M., and Dhillon, S. (2017). *Impact of TNTP's teaching fellows in urban school districts*, American Institutes for Research.

229   Sims, S. (2018). *What happens when you pay shortage-subject teachers more money? Simulating the effect of early-career salary supplements on teacher supply in England.* Report for Gatsby Foundation.

230   E.g. through evidence-based policies to reallocate teachers such as this: Glazerman, S., Protik, A., Teh, B., Bruch, J., and Max, J. (2013). *Transfer incentives for high-performing teachers: Final results from a multisite randomized experiment*, Institute of Education Sciences Report.

Or through evidence-based policies to improve leadership and therefore retention, such as this:

Knibbs, S., Mollidor, C., Lindley, L., Allen, R., and Sims, S. (2017). *High potential middle leaders (secondary) programme: An evaluation.* London: National College for Teaching & Leadership.

231   Tierney, S. (2017, 19 November). *Teacher monitoring: Lessons from pig wrestling* [Blog post]. Retrieved from: https://leadinglearner. me/2017/11/19/teacher-monitoring-lessons-from-pig-wrestling.

INDEX

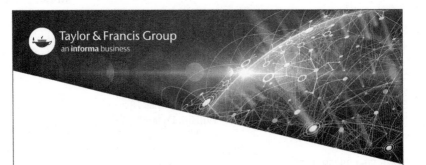